St Thomas of Hereford

To Kit

Also by Gabriel Alington

The Hereford Mappa Mundi
Borderlands

St Thomas of Hereford

GABRIEL ALINGTON

illustrations by
DOMINIC HARBOUR

First published in 2001

Gracewing
2 Southern Avenue, Leominster
Herefordshire HR6 0QF

Cover photographs of the Seal of Bishop Thomas Cantilupe and the Shrine of St Thomas: © The Dean and Chapter of Hereford Cathedral.

ISBN 0 85244 525 3

Typeset by Action Publishing Technology Ltd,
Gloucester GL1 5SR

Printed by MPG Books Ltd.,
Bodmin PL31 1EG

FOREWORD

St Thomas of Hereford was the major saint of the Cathedral Church in Hereford throughout the years of the later Middle Ages. His shrine replaced that of the shrine of St Ethelbert which had been totally destroyed in the disaster of 1055. Pilgrims began to flock to the shrine of St Thomas and, miraculously, because of the removal of the shrine to the Lady Chapel, the earlier shrine has survived. Recently, at the end of the major stage of restoration of the Cantilupe shrine, our Cathedral Archivist found in the archives the complete list of monastic houses and hostelries which St Thomas and his retinue used on the last journey across Europe to Rome. The neat list includes amounts spent and gives a fascinating picture of life in the thirteenth century. Despite Thomas Cantilupe's enormous importance both spiritually and politically in medieval England, not much has been told about him or commonly known about him in recent years. Now, however, with the restoration of the shrine such a book as this is very timely.

With a fascinating wealth of detail Gabriel Alington has given us a picture not only of the man himself but also of the social and political context in which his life was lived. The book brings to life a crucial time in the history of the Cathedral Church of Hereford, and tells clearly and attractively the story of this episcopal saint. I hope that those reading it will not only find the story of interest for its own sake, portraying the all-too-human qualities of the influential prelate and politician, but also will find that their knowledge of the cathedral itself is enhanced.

As a Foundation we are immensely grateful for all the work that has been put into this very attractive biography.

Robert Willis
Dean of Hereford

INTRODUCTION

Gabriel Alington has used her skill with the pen to give us a lively and absorbing account of Thomas of Hereford. Seven hundred years ago the campaign for his canonization was in full swing, building upon the fact that pilgrims from all over the country were visiting his shrine in the cathedral in Hereford to seek cures or blessings either for themselves or their loved ones. Recently work has been completed on a restoration of the shrine, one of the few remaining intact in England. The work included not only the preservation of the stonework but also the clearing of the space around the site in the north transept so that its beauty and significance could be fully appreciated. As is explained in the following pages, a much more elaborate shrine was built in the Lady Chapel in the fourteenth century, after Thomas had been declared a saint, of which nothing remains. But by that time the cult was well past its peak. The great majority of the claimed miracles of healing which Gabriel recounts took place at this spot, or at least during the period when the bones of Thomas lay buried here.

During the work on restoring the shrine the cathedral archivist, Rosalind Caird, identified a document as the account roll for Thomas's final journey to Italy, described in chapter ten. This enabled his exact route to be identified. Suddenly Thomas stepped out of the shadows and began to take on once again the dimensions of this world. Now this book continues this process and gives the reader a vivid insight into the age in which Thomas lived and what it was like for a person in his situation to work out his vocation to be 'in the world, but not of it'. Our world today is very different, but at the start of a new millennium we need stories from our Christian past to focus for us afresh the call to holiness, goodness and truth which must be heeded if the followers of our Lord Jesus Christ are to be 'the salt of the earth'. In what follows, Thomas Cantilupe stands before us as a truly 'salty' character.

John Tiller

ACKNOWLEDGEMENTS

I am most grateful to Robert Willis, Dean of Hereford, and Canon John Tiller for so generously contributing to this book, also to Canon James Butterworth whose idea it was in the first place. I would also like to thank Bishop John Saxbee for his helpful information on border parishes, and Rosalind Caird and Joan Williams for their patient help with my research. I am greatly indebted to John Ross for supplying me with much original material concerning the miracles and giving his time to discuss them with me. I would also like to thank Michael Hooper, Archdeacon of Hereford, Father Illtud Barrett, David Annett and George Alderson for their interest and help with Catholicism, churches and heraldry, as well as Peter Holliday, Angela Davies and the other staff at Leominster Public Library for their patient and enthusiastic assistance. I am everlastingly grateful to Jo Ashworth for all her hard work in the production of this book, and, lastly to my husband, Peter, for his invaluable help and for so good-naturedly putting up with my long preoccupation.

CHAPTER I

Thomas Cantilupe stood out among the leaders of his age, a man of exceptional character; selfless, discerning, courageous and deeply spiritual. He was not only Hereford's most famous bishop, he was Chancellor of England, twice Chancellor of Oxford University; in 1320, thirty-eight years after his death, he was canonized. Yet now, and for many centuries, few beyond Hereford have heard of him.

Not far from Hereford, in the south wall of the chancel of Credenhill church is a small stained glass window dating from about 1310. In it two figures stand side by side, Becket, the martyred Archbishop of Canterbury, and Bishop Cantilupe of Hereford, both named Thomas, both revered as saints. And there were other similarities; both were staunch defenders of the rights of the church, both held high office in church and state, both, following their deaths, at once became the centre of a cult,[1] attracting pilgrims to their respective shrines. So for a time, while both cults flourished, their names were linked. But whereas Becket's fame continued right

1

through the Middle Ages – his martyrdom had caught the spirit of the time, church and people against the crown, and spread throughout Europe – the cult of Cantilupe, never so widespread, did not retain popular support beyond the mid-fourteenth century. In any case, though there are parallels between their lives, they are largely superficial, little more than coincidence. Dig deeper and you find they had little in common; their backgrounds were different, their education and their academic standing; there was nothing to compare in the manner of their deaths, very little in their claims to sancitity. The most significant, the most fundamental difference, was in their personalities.

Almost all we know of Thomas Cantilupe the man comes from the evidence given by witnesses at the enquiry for his canonization in 1307. These records, the words of elderly servants and friends who had been close to him in life, show us something of the way he lived, his priorities, his habits, his character.

Until 1982, the 700th anniversary of Cantilupe's death, when a book of essays on different aspects of his life was published in his honour, the only biography was *The Life and Gests of Saint Thomas* by a seventeenth-century Jesuit, Richard Strange.[2] Strange eulogizes Thomas, portraying him as the personification of purity and austerity, but telling us little else. The foreword of a nineteenth-century reprint of his book describes the work as 'full of unction but somewhat meagre in fact ...' Like the book of essays, Strange's biography is based on the records of the canonization process.

The year of Thomas's birth is generally believed to have been 1218 though recent research suggests it may have been four years later.[3] Either way he was

2

born at a time of change, a turbulent time when the subjects of the crown were challenging its monopoly of power, when the barons, for the most part united, were demanding rights established by law. These, set out in Magna Carta, had been granted at Runnymede by King John. He had failed to keep his word; within months there had been further conflict, then civil war. Yet the first Magna Carta had been a beginning, a breakthrough for the rights of the people, albeit the people who owned wealth and land, the powerful aristocracy. But the seed had been sown; there was no going back.

There must have been a feeling in the air, a hunger for freedom and basic rights. And perhaps, as an infant, Thomas Cantilupe breathed it in, for as he grew up he came to believe in such a code of government, to believe in it passionately, almost, you could say, instinctively. Though not only for the barons, the men of power; his creed was justice for everyone, peasant, craftsman, merchant, lord. Justice, yet not equality. There was no such thing in those feudal times. Class or status was a fact of life. No one questioned it. You were born a peasant or a nobleman, and though some bought their freedom, moved into towns and improved their lot, they would never expect to do more than that.

Thomas Cantilupe's own background was distinctly aristocratic. Both his parents were descended from Norman barons. His father, William, second Baron Cantilupe, was seneschal, or steward, of the royal household, an office held by his own father before him. His mother, Millicent, the daughter of the Norman lord, Hugh de Gournay, was the widow of the Count of Evreux, Amauri de Montfort. The de Montfort connection was reinforced by the close friendship of Thomas's uncle, Walter Cantilupe, later Bishop of Worcester, with Simon de Montfort, the Earl of Leicester.

The name Cantilupe is thought to be derived from the French *champs de loup*, field of the wolf. Different versions of Cantilupe can be found as a place name in northern France; Chantelou, Chantaloube, Canteleu, and there are many more, as well as Aston-Cantlow, the family seat in Warwickshire. The Cantilupe arms, which incidentally was adopted by the Diocese of Hereford, shows fleur-de-lys, their family blazon, above reversed leopards' heads. Alternatively it has been argued that the heads are those of wolves, or 'cantrels', and that the fleur-de-lys represents spears impaling the heads.

Thomas was one of a large family; we know that at least eight children survived infancy, five boys and three girls. Thomas had two elder brothers, William, who became the third Baron Cantilupe, and Hugh, who went into the church. John and Nicholas, probably younger than Thomas, both became knights. Of his sisters, he seems to have been closest to Juliana, who is thought to have been next to him in age and so his childhood companion. In adult life they continued to keep in touch, particularly after Thomas became Bishop of Hereford, for Juliana, who like her sisters married into noble families, was by then the wife of Robert de Tregoz of Ewyas, one of the Marcher lords. When she heard the news of her brother's appointment she was so delighted that she decided to go in person to congratulate him, riding the seven leagues from Ewyas, roughly twenty-two miles, to his manor house at Bosbury, through wild and thickly wooded countryside.

A story told by two of the witnesses at the canonization hearings recounts how, as Juliana came forward to greet him, Thomas held out his hand for her to kiss. Juliana showed surprise; she appeared disconcerted, even distressed, for others who were present urged Thomas to embrace her as it seems he had always done before. They reminded him that it was customary in England for a bishop to kiss members of his family; there was really no harm. Still Thomas refused, no doubt gently; he would never have deliberately hurt his sister's feelings. And although the historian, T. F. Tout describes Juliana as mortally wounded by the rebuff, it may rather be that, knowing him so well, she understood his gesture was not a rebuff but a sign of his episcopal authority, a sign that in his new role he felt it right to observe extreme chastity. Which may strike us as overdoing it, piety carried a touch too far. But this was an age when every female, even a dear sister, was considered a temptress, a naturally wayward and fickle creature, best kept at arm's length by men of God.[4]

The Cantilupe family home, where Thomas was born, was the manor house of Hambleden, four miles from Great Marlow in Buckinghamshire, and it is probably there, in the village church, that Thomas was christened. How much of his early childhood he spent at Hambleden we do not know. It was the custom for baronial households to move from place to place, visiting their various manors and castles, and the length of their stay was apt to depend on the state of the drains. When the smell of sewage became unbearable the whole entourage would pack up and move on. Parents naturally did their best to have their children brought up in a healthy situation, *ipso facto* where the drains functioned effectively. Considering the number of Cantilupe babies who survived infancy, Hambleden, six miles north of the Thames, must have been blessed with well-sluiced drains. So it seems likely that much of Thomas's early years were spent there, in the Buckinghamshire country-side.

It is also likely that he and his siblings saw little of their parents, certainly their father, who, as seneschal to the royal household would have been continually involved in the service of the king. And the king, in this case the young Henry III, with his enormous retinue of servants and officials, was constantly trav-elling round his kingdom.

In fact this separation of children from their parents was the custom among the nobility. Lady Cantilupe would have handed over each newborn infant to a nurse, a wet nurse at first, carefully chosen and preferably one who had herself borne sons; proof of her commendable qualities – so it was believed.

In his biography of Cantilupe, Richard Strange refers to Thomas's nurse as a 'noble matron', though whether she was noble in character or social standing is not clear; perhaps she was both. Or perhaps, which would seem to make most sense, a 'noble matron' took over from the wet nurse when Thomas had been weaned and this more educated woman would have also acted as his governess until he reached the age of seven or eight. Whoever she was, this 'noble matron', her influence, would seem to have been good. At a guess she was calm, understanding, firm, and instilled in small Thomas a sense of obedience, truth-fulness and self control.

The belief at that time, according to the works of theologians such as Bernard of Clairvaux[5] and Anselm of Canterbury,[6] was that children should be nurtured with gentleness and love. Babies should be swaddled securely, though not too tightly; they should not be left to cry but should be soothed with lullabies, 'sung in a pleasant and harmonious voice'. This advice came from the twelfth-century philosopher, Adelard of Bath, who believed that harsh discordant sounds could cause lasting harm. And while children should always be treated kindly there should be no sparing of the rod.[7] Medieval society was far more violent and physical than our politically correct age so that for serious naughtiness beating, even whipping, provided it was carefully controlled, was recommended by writers such as the late twelfth-century French philosopher, William of Auvergne.[8] And, though too late to influence Thomas's upbringing, his close contemporary, the great Dominican theologian, Thomas Aquinas, considered suffering to be an integral part of the teaching of good qualities.

Less physical, yet perhaps as effective, was the threat of the Devil who, in that age, was as real to adults as to their charges. Children would be warned that this fire-breathing monster might suddenly appear and snatch them away to the underworld. But there was also forgiveness, on condition of repentance, for which Thomas would have learned the appropriate prayers as soon as he could talk. His nurse, or perhaps Lady Cantilupe, would have taught him to recite the three most important, the *Paternoster*, *Credo* and *Ave Maria*, also how to cross himself reverently. He would too have been taken to Mass, said early each morning in the family chapel and attended by the household.[9]

The main meal of the day was usually served between 10 and 11 a.m. and, once Thomas was old enough, he would have taken his place at table in the great hall of the manor. As a rule the lord and lady with their family sat at the main table, sometimes on a raised dais, while the retainers ate at trestle tables below. Thomas would have learned that, during meals, it was wrong to belch, to pick his nose or to wipe it on his napkin; nor should he cram so much into his mouth he could not answer when spoken to, or return half-chewed food to the communal dish. This last must refer mainly to meat, most of which, being decidedly free range, was extremely tough. The households of feudal lords ate great quantities of meat: beef, venison, lamb, wild boar, as well as birds such as pigeons, peacocks, gulls. Whole carcasses were roasted on a spit, or cut up and stewed with herbs and spices to disguise the often high and rancid taste. To accompany the meat there was always bread, big chunks of it, some of which would be put in the base of the dish to soak up the juices. During Lent, when the Church forbade the eating of meat, fish was served instead, probably from the manor's well-stocked ponds, also when the Cantilupes were at Hambleden, from the Thames. Lampreys[10] were popular cooked in a variety of ways, a galantine perhaps, with raisins, vinegar and crusts of bread, and according to a medieval recipe, 'added thereto powder gynger and ye bloode and ye greece ...'

Thomas was particularly fond of a pie made with lampreys from the river Severn, so much so that, as a priest, he would deny himself this treat. At the canonization hearings his servant, Hugh le Barber, described, revealingly, how the lord Thomas would have the lamprey pie brought before him, then he would ask if it were well done, then he would lean close savouring the smell. And then he would have it put aside for others to eat.

From the kitchen garden belonging to the manor would come vegetables; leeks, onions, cabbage, beans – potatoes were unknown in England at that time – and, from the orchards, fruits; apples, plums, pears. For young children the meat would be pounded into a mush then mixed with milk. Honey, the only form of sweetening, was combined with almonds, eggs and milk to make puddings suitable for the nursery.

Small children were encouraged to play. Writers on the upbringing of children, basing their advice on philosophers such as Aristotle, who believed in the unity of mind and body, emphasized its importance. The thirteenth-century scholar, Philip of Novare, considered that nature demanded play.[11]

Baby Thomas would have started his play with a rattle made of wood or bone, moved on to building blocks, piling them up then galloping round them on his hobby horse; he would have learned to throw a ball, bowl a hoop, toot on a whistle and beat a drum. With his nurse he would first have played pat-a-cake, then, with his siblings, blindman's buff, or hoodman's blind, as well as skipping, singing and dancing games. On fine days the children would have played outside, rocking on a see-saw, sailing boats on the manor pond and probably, when still quite small, Thomas and his brothers would have learned to ride. More difficult skills such as fencing and tilting would have come later as part of their formal education.

As a rule this did not begin until the age of seven though in some cases boys of five or six – girls were educated quite differently – would begin to learn Latin and Norman French. Possibly Thomas, intelligent and quick to learn – 'with a mind full of generous heat and vigour' as Richard Strange puts it –

would have started lessons with either a tutor or the household chaplain.

With few exceptions scholarly and religious works were written in Latin while Norman French, the language spoken by the aristocracy, was increasingly used for romantic verse.

The Arthurian legends, tales of chivalry[12] threaded with magic, were highly popular in medieval times, with adults as well as children, and from an early age Thomas would have been familiar with them. There were many different versions. In the *Historia Regum Britanniae*, by the twelfth-century chronicler, Geoffrey of Monmouth, Arthur appears as a heroic figure born at Tintagel, who, crowned king of Britain at the age of fifteen, set up court at Camelot in Somerset, won many battles and married Guinevere. The Welsh, however, claimed Arthur as their compatriot, a sixth-century leader who held court at Caerleon and would one day return to lead them to victory. For a small boy these legends were the stuff of dreams, the inspiration for play, for make-believe. In his games he could have imagined himself as Arthur, Lancelot or Galahad; perhaps with Juliana as Guinevere.

And, from time to time, when a band of minstrels called at the Cantilupe manor, Thomas would have heard versions of the legends played and sung by these itinerant musicians, who travelled round the country offering entertainment. As a rule a band would announce their arrival by singing a chorus outside the walls, hoping to be invited in. Once admitted they would group themselves at one end of the hall, or on the minstrel's gallery, with their instruments; clarions, pipes, tambours, gitterns, and the early viols, rebecs and vielles played with an arc-shaped bow. Sometimes there would also be mummers, tumblers, jugglers, even dancing bears. But generally the entertainment would consist mainly of music, ballads with themes of chivalry and romantic love, the Arthurian legend told in song.

It is possible also that, when still young, Thomas watched jousting in the 'lists', a long enclosure divided by a 'tilt', or fence. These contests when two knights would charge towards each other on either side of the tilt, each aiming his lance at the other's shield, while on a far smaller scale than a full-blown tournament, were still spectacular and risky and probably as exciting to a thirteenth-century six-year-old as a World Cup football match to today's small boy. Exciting and inspiring? Though whether it was watching knights in action, hearing tales of chivalry and knightly deeds, or simply making believe he was a knight himself, that fired Thomas's ambition, we shall never know. Whatever the reason, when still quite small, he made up his mind. When asked what he would be when he grew up, without hesitation he announced that he was going to be a soldier, a knight at arms.

CHAPTER II

'You shall indeed be a soldier,' Walter Cantilupe told his young nephew when he heard of Thomas's ambition, 'a soldier to serve the King of Kings under the banner of His blessed martyr, Saint Thomas of Canterbury.'

Which sounds heartily avuncular but also categorical. As if the matter had been settled. As if that was that.

Richard Strange claims that Thomas 'thought no more of these glorious fancies'. Whether that is true or whether, boldly, he pointed out to his uncle that he could very well serve the King of Kings by being a crusader and fighting for Christ in the Holy Land, he would not have got far. The implication that small Thomas should serve under the banner of his namesake was clear. Like his elder brother, Hugh, he was to go into the church. His early education would be guided by his uncle, Walter.

According to Richard Strange, Thomas remained at Hambleden with his 'pious parents' throughout his childhood. Which may be so. On the other hand it was far more usual for sons of the nobility, aged

13

seven or eight, to be handed over to another family, possibly relations but certainly of similar status. By then a boy's future would have been decided; an eldest son would inherit the title while younger sons would either train for knighthood or the church, as a secular priest or to join a monastic order.

Walter Cantilupe seems to have taken a particular interest in his nephew, Thomas. Perhaps he saw in the small redhead, who was clearly intelligent – in Strange's words had 'a mind full of generous heat and vigour' – the promise of something exceptional. Perhaps, privately, Thomas was to him, the son who, as a celibate priest, he would never have. Children must have been important to him for, like his contemporary, Robert Grosseteste,[1] Bishop of Lincoln, he wrote practical advice on caring for the young; mothers were warned against overlaying babies, to guard against cradles being upset or left close to water or fire.

It may be that Walter Cantilupe persuaded his elder brother and sister-in-law that he should act as Thomas's mentor and train him for the church; more likely the decision was mutual. In the thirteenth century the church was extremely powerful. To have a son who held high office, who was able to exercise patronage, would, in future, be of great advantage. And guided by Walter Cantilupe Thomas would surely do well.

He must have been impressively able, young Walter Cantilupe. In 1227, having recently graduated from either Paris or Oxford, he was sent on behalf of Henry III on a mission to the Roman Curia, the papal court. Four years later as a justice in eyre (a circuit judge) he was a junior partner to two of the most prominent clerical judges, William Raleigh and

Martin of Pattishall. He then rose higher still to become a Royal Justice. In 1236 he was elected Bishop of Worcester, an appointment readily approved by both Henry III and Pope Gregory IX. A hefty loan, possibly as much as a thousand marks, was made available from the royal wardrobe to cover the expenses of his journey to Rome for consecration. Walter believed strongly in plurality, the holding of numerous benefices, and spoke out effectively in its defence at a council in London in 1237. How else, he argued, could a churchman of his status live in suitable style? To be fair this included donations to charity as well as generous hospitality. Indeed Walter Cantilupe was highly regarded, the greatest bishop of his time some claimed. But always the exception was the Bishop of Lincoln, Robert Grosseteste,[2] who before becoming a bishop had taught at Oxford, who was a brilliant and innovative scientist, knowledgeable in physics, astronomy, optics, mathematics and more besides. Walter Cantilupe could never compete with that. Nor would he have tried. The two were friends, like-minded over several controversial issues, papal taxation, for example, which they supported against the crown.

Walter Cantilupe, a leading Montfortian, was a close friend of Simon de Montfort, backing him fully in the Baron's War against the King. Which was why it was said, after his death, he never came to be canonized.

It was probably about 1225 that Thomas, aged seven, began his education under Walter's guidance. As Master Robert of Gloucester, who later became Thomas's companion and secretary, put it, Walter Cantilupe 'sent his nephew to the schools and beneficed him'. But which schools? It is possible that in the mid 1220s, Walter, having recently graduated, was an Oxford master, in which case Thomas would have lived with him there and been steeped in an atmosphere of learning. It was a time when the thirst for knowledge was growing, when new ideas on the arts, the natural sciences, theology, philosophy, were crystallising, firing men's imaginations, exciting them. The first encyclopaedias were being produced, massive works such as *De natura rerum* by Alexander Nequam and *De proprietatibus rerum* by Bartolomaeus Anglicus; English law, influenced by Roman concept of justice, was developing and being framed.

At first Thomas would have been too young to comprehend much of this high intellect, but possibly he would have found the atmosphere contagious, have been curious, questioned, wondered. And surely Walter Cantilupe, however involved in other matters, would have made time for Thomas, to teach and encourage him, to stretch his mind. Probably too, Walter, being young himself, would have taken Thomas out for exercise; together they would have gone riding, hunting perhaps for deer and boar, or hawking with a falcon – the sport of the aristocracy – through the wooded countryside of Oxfordshire.

At this stage, under Walter's guidance, Thomas is likely to have had his own tutor, possibly the chaplain of the household. Alternatively, being destined for the church, he may have attended a choir school or 'song school', as they were sometimes called. These, unlike the more secular grammar schools, were attached to an abbey or cathedral with the children forming part of the choir and a syllabus which included singing and religious music. Otherwise, as in grammar schools, children would study Latin and Norman French, reading, scripture and arithmetic.

Though some writing was taught it was mainly rated a technical skill to be carried out by scribes and was not part of general education. Over the age of twelve other subjects studied might be rhetoric, dialectics (the art of logical debate), some science and astrology.

As far as Thomas is concerned all this is speculation; there is no known record of his early education. But wherever he received it, whatever it included, it must surely have been thorough and comprehensive, in the true sense of the word. So that when, in 1237, at the age of about nineteen, he went to Oxford University 'to be initiated in Academical learning' as the seventeenth-century historian, Anthony Wood,[3] puts it, he was well able to get to grips with his studies.

His chief tutor at Oxford was the Dominican, Robert Kilwardby, whom Richard Strange describes as 'a great person' chosen 'by the special Providence of God' to be Thomas's 'spiritual guide and governor'. Strange got it right. Kilwardby must indeed have been a great person for he was to become Prior Provincial of the English Dominicans; he was later nominated by Pope Gregory X to be Archbishop of Canterbury; eventually he rose to be a cardinal. He was also Thomas's lifelong friend, 'a particular friend' as Hugh le Barber, Thomas's servant, put it in his canonization evidence.

Kilwardby was a Master of Arts of Paris University and we know that, after three or four years at Oxford, Thomas followed in his footsteps, moving to Paris to join his brother, Hugh, in studying for an arts degree.

Paris, founded about 1170, was one of Europe's oldest universities – only Salerno and Bologna were earlier. The founding of Oxford University may have resulted from the barring of English students from Paris at the end of the twelfth century. In time however *entente* was recovered and well before Thomas's day the two universities had become closely linked; students moved freely from one to the other and could take the same degrees. Among the famous professors who taught at both universities were Alexander of Hales, who came from Gloucestershire, the Italian Saint Bonaventure and although there is no record of the Dominican, Thomas Aquinas, lecturing at Oxford, he was certainly one of the great masters in Paris at that time.

Paris University had grown out of the cathedral schools of Notre Dame and, as at most medieval universities, lectures and classes were held in halls and churches with the majority of students living in endowed boarding-houses. These were primarily intended for impoverished MAs and BAs to enable them to stay on and take a higher degree; in fact they were shared with undergraduates, most of whom were also impoverished.

The atmosphere of university life in those days was far from the serenity of traditional dreaming spires. This was particularly true of Paris, situated at the heart of the city which, in the Middle Ages, was the hub of northern Europe; a great metropolis where travellers of all kinds, merchants, pilgrims, friars and crusaders, jostled with the city dwellers, the burghers, tradesmen, beggars and students, along the narrow streets. The thirteenth-century Hereford Mappa Mundi, which marks each town and city with a building relative to its size, shows Paris as a grand turreted cathedral dwarfing all others in that part of the world.

Thomas and Hugh did not lodge in a boarding house; they were noblemen. They shared a residence suited to their status, with numerous servants and their personal chaplain. They also brought with them their own tutor, Master Peter de Buttevilt, who was later steward to Walter Cantilupe at Worcester.

The brothers lived in grand style, keeping what is known as a good table and, according to Thomas's servant, Hugh le Barber, were sociable and hospitable to all ranks of men. Hugh le Barber, who had not known Thomas then himself, had heard this from Master de Buttevilt, also Dom William Daubeney, another member of the household. They had recounted how, in 1242, no less a person than Saint Louis, King of France, had visited the brothers, how, at the other end of the scale, the servants were instructed to save all leftover food and give it to paupers, to beggars on the streets, a crowd of whom were probably camped permanently outside the house.

Without the university custom of dining in hall,[4] meals in the houses of wealthy scholars were not only a time to be sociable but a time for talk, for serious discussion. When so much of learning relied on debate, the airing of ideas, it was bound to be so. Thomas would have been happy with that but when, perhaps towards the end of a meal, conversation gave way to exuberance, to wild behaviour and ribaldry, he would not have taken part. Again according to Hugh le Barber, Thomas was averse to smutty humour and bawdy songs. Indeed so openly did he show his dislike it was said that he should have been a woman rather than a man. His unworldliness was another cause for comment. He was known to have had sometimes to borrow money. But what nobleman would carry coins? And at one stage he was labelled a *rusticus*, a country bumpkin. A country man, yes, but the stately and patrician Thomas was scarcely a bumpkin. Streetwise, however, he was not.

But perhaps such aspersions were kept low key, voiced out of ear-shot, noted discreetly with looks and nods, for the Cantilupe hospitality was extended to their fellow students many of whom, being penniless, were thankful for a meal. Open criticism could have soured their welcome. And for a number of the poorest scholars there was lodging too, as well as pocket money to supply their needs.

In any case, though many students were rough and unruly, very few were not ambitious, eager to learn, ultimately to obtain a degree; that was why they were there.

According to regulations laid down in 1215 the arts course required six years of study followed by two further years of lecturing in the faculty, or what was known as the 'necessary regency', the particular department of learning. Possibly by around 1240, when the Cantilupes were studying in Paris, the regulations had been relaxed. What is known for sure is the composition of the course; arithmetic, geometry, astronomy, grammar, logic, music, rhetoric, seven subjects studied in depth. Somehow six years of learning, merely six, does not seem so long.

Generally the course was based on ancient learning, on the works of philosophers, such as Aristotle and Plato who belonged, respectively, to the fourth and fifth centuries BC. The doctrines of Plato, or rather Platonism, became interwoven with early Christian theology so was highly regarded in the early church, unlike the teaching of Aristotle which was thought to lead to a materialistic outlook on life; his works on natural science were strongly condemned. But in the 1230s Aristotle's ideas came back into favour and the translations of his writings by Arabic scholars of the eleventh and twelfth centuries, Avicenna and Averroes, the 'new Aristotle', were accepted universally. Aristotle was in. Certainly his approach of open-minded enquiry with only an outline solution provided, fitted well with the method of teaching practised in Paris. Following a lecture a class of students, directed by their master, would take sides to debate the ideas put forward, questioning, discussing, dissecting, analysing each point in detail. The students were encouraged to be critical, to view accepted theories from a sceptical and original slant. Debates would grow heated; they were intensely involving and would last for many hours, even days.

Another reason for this method of learning was the rarity of books. In the twelfth and thirteenth centuries a textbook was a massive compendium known as a *summa* which set out comprehensive instruction on a particular subject and generally in a similar form of debate, enquiry followed by affirmation and contra-diction. There was, after all, so much to question; in philosophy, in science, in astronomy; for example the shape of the zodiac, the influence of its various signs; Cancer, Aries, Capricorn, the number of planets, the number of worlds . . .

In 1245 Thomas and Hugh went together to the First Council of Lyons. This major ecumenical meeting was convened by Pope Innocent IV, to rally forces against the Emperor. Frederick II, a brilliant and arrogant man – he was known as *stupor mundi* – was extremely hostile to the Pope. The chronicler, Matthew Paris, had noted four years earlier that Frederick, whom he referred to as the new Lucifer or Anti-Christ, was in league with the Tartars for the subversion of the Christian faith.

For Thomas and Hugh the summit, the first time either had attended a public event, was a landmark occasion. It was an opportunity for them to meet and, with their royal connections, to be accepted by the magnates of the church. These were men who wielded power and influence. In the Middle Ages cardinals and bishops were not only leaders within the church, they were closely involved in the affairs of state: many had earlier been statesmen themselves and had attained their positions by royal favour. To know them mattered, to have their friendship mattered considerably more.

The Cantilupes made a good impression. The Pope remarked on their learning, their nobility and elegance of manner. He gave them both the title of papal chaplain, appointed Thomas to be a prebend at Saint Paul's in London and granted him a dispensation allowing him to hold livings in plurality (to be the priest of more than one living). Travelling back to Paris the brothers must have felt they had the world at their feet. To have received such honours – Thomas, in particular, had reason to feel proud to have done so well.

Or perhaps, resisting hubris, he simply felt blessed.

It may be, as the historian, Jeremy Catto, suggests, that Thomas's next move was influenced by his meeting with the Pope. Innocent IV, who with his powerful leadership would have made a strong impression on Thomas, had previously taught canon law at Bologna University. Perhaps Thomas hoped to follow his example for, having completed the arts course, he set off for Orleans, this time without Hugh, to study law. There were two complementary legal systems, Roman, on which civil law was based, and canon. Thomas started with canon law.[5]

Until the early thirteenth century Paris had been the centre for the study of Roman law, but the French king, Philip Augustus, had grown uneasy about the power attributed to the Emperor Otto by Roman lawyers. When, in 1214, a combined force led by the Emperor defeated the French at the battle of Bouvines, Philip Augustus had had enough. He banned the study of Roman law in Paris and expelled all who taught it. The masters headed south for the recently established University of Orleans where they set up the centre for the study of civil law. By the time Thomas arrived in 1246 it had been formally recognized by a papal bull and was flourishing.

We know from Robert of Gloucester that Thomas was taught law by Master Guido. This was Guido de Guinis, a highly distinguished and innovative lawyer, who had himself been trained in Bologna by two of the leading legal figures of his day. Guido was the first known Doctor of Law at a French university, and from his surviving works, it is clear that he played a major part in reconciling the differences between the Italian and French legal systems; the long-established school of Roman law with its emphasis on juridical principle with the more practical French approach concentrating on procedure and the customary law of each locality.

It must be, too, that Master Guido was a gifted teacher for it was not long before Thomas had such a grasp of the subject that he was able to take over, often giving lectures in place of Guido, acting as master, while, as he did so, gearing himself for his future life.

Some years later, probably about 1252, Thomas returned to Paris to round off his legal studies with canon law. Hugh, who had remained there, was by then reading theology – he later became Archdeacon of Gloucester – but this time the brothers lived separately, doubtless each with a household suited to their status and, certainly in Thomas's case, continuing to offer hospitality to rich and poor.

Canon law, the law of the church, was set out according to the same principles as Roman law. A decade earlier the great master of canon law, Henry of Susa, who later became known as Hostiensis, had taught at Paris University. Hostiensis established a broader, more flexible interpretation of canon law, one based more on ethics, on moral principle, than the rigid approach of previous times drawn from sources in scripture and early theologians.[7] Thomas is bound to have been influenced by this, to have built on it in later years when, as a bishop, he would judge each issue independently, as he saw right.

At last in 1255, or thereabouts, Thomas, now bachelor of canon law, came home to England for the final stage of his education, a doctorate in canon law at Oxford. It was in the same year that both his father and his eldest brother, William, died, and it could be that their deaths influenced his decision to return. Perhaps, though not next in line for the title, he felt he should be on hand to take some responsibility for the family affairs. Apart from that he may have wanted to go back to his old university, which by now had grown in size and, due to the generosity of patrons, one of them Walter Cantilupe, had also become richer and more fashionable. University College had been founded six years before and was soon to be followed by Balliol. The Franciscans and Dominicans had established schools in Oxford and, particularly the Franciscans, had produced outstanding scholars; William of Ockham, Adam Marsh and most brilliant of all, Roger Bacon. Under Grosseteste's tuition, Bacon studied heat and light, made telescopes and explosives, even, it was said, designed self-powered chariots and flying machines. As a centre of learning Oxford was no longer second to Paris. Indeed as far as law was concerned, Oxford, where both civil and canon law were taught – the two were closely connected – was superior to Paris, where the faculty of civil (Roman) law no longer existed.

During the three years of study for his doctorate Thomas is likely to have concentrated on the procedural and practical side of canon law, attending lectures based on William of Drogheda's *Summa Aurea*, a guide on the procedure of church courts by the man who had been a master at Oxford when Thomas had first been there. Such knowledge would be vital for those who, like Thomas, were aiming for high office in the church.

Records show that 1257, the second year of Thomas's Oxford studies, was disastrously wet. For month after month, through spring then summer it rained ceaselessly. Unripe fruit rotted on the trees, sodden corn remained uncut. It may be that Thomas, deep in his studies, was not affected, not at first. But come the autumn when the crops still lay flattened in the fields the threat of famine was increasingly real. Bishops gave permission for everyone, including college students, to work on Sundays and holy days salvaging the harvest. But it was past saving. That winter people resorted to eating horseflesh and bark, the wheat price rocketed from two shillings a quarter to an incredible twenty shillings, even twenty-four.[8] Thomas could afford to pay that price for wheat but whatever he bought as well as any other food he had, he would have shared with those who most needed it.

In 1258, after over two decades of concentrated study, he finally received his doctorate and for the next three years he remained at Oxford to teach canon law. He must have done so successfully; he knew his subject inside out, he was authoritative, he was certainly an excellent administrator, abilities which, added together, were those of a natural leader. And at forty he must have felt ready to become one, to hold a position of authority. Besides which he was a nobleman with friends in high places. At one point, while at Oxford, he invited Prince Edward with many magnates and justices, to a feast in London. Perhaps it was to mark a particular occasion or simply hospitality on a fitting scale. And though apparently King Henry did not attend the feast, it seems he counted Thomas as a friend, sending him a gift of royal oaks as a mark of favour.

So it cannot have come as a great surprise when in 1261 Thomas was elected Chancellor of the University.

As Chancellor, a post established in 1214, Thomas was both the head of the congregation of masters, who formed the governing body, and its judge with criminal, civil and spiritual jurisdiction. As Richard Strange puts it, he was the head 'not only in Doctrine but also in moral discipline and comportment both of masters and students'. Two masters were elected annually as proctors with responsibility for keeping the peace. Which from the sound of it was asking a good deal of only two men.

From the beginning there had been considerable rivalry between the university and the town. At times this would result in riots, physical violence. Thomas tackled this diplomatically by arranging to meet the burgesses of the town, possibly wining and dining them, mellowing their mood. The outcome was that the burgesses agreed to swear on oath to the university statutes. Perhaps the more far-sighted saw the likely advantage of being lined up behind a leading supporter of the increasingly powerful Simon de Montfort.[9]

But trouble in the main came from within the university. The number of students was growing rapidly with many freshmen from areas far from Oxford, from what then were thought of as 'foreign parts'. Local students resented the outcomers, uncouth northerners most of all, and, as all scholars were allowed to carry arms, any insult or quarrel would escalate, often ending in injury, even death. According to Hugh le Barber, Thomas dealt severely with troublesome students, confiscating their arms, in some cases permanently. Hugh, who had not then been at Oxford with Thomas, remembered later seeing a positive armoury of confiscated weapons, at least twenty confiscated bows as well as numerous long and short swords. He had himself been given, presumably by Thomas, a long sword removed from a particularly unruly student called Roger de Horn. Hugh le Barber had heard how successful Thomas was as Chancellor, how just and wise he proved himself. And, in his flowery style, Richard Strange echoes this, recounting how Thomas 'demeaned himself with such uprightness and integrity that he never swerved from the path of truth'.

On one occasion while Thomas was Chancellor – it was during Lent when it was said 'quarrels were easily begun' – a confrontation took place between two student gangs, southerners and northerners, who named themselves the Australes and Boreales. As the fighting flared, spread, grew violent, and the proctors lost control, Thomas appeared on the scene. A tall figure, alone, unarmed, protected only by his cloak,

27

he pushed his way to the middle of the fight. In the moments before the mobsters were aware who was now among them, he was caught between the flailing fists and swords; his cloak was slashed. He must have been battered, bruised and cut; miraculously there was nothing worse; by the grace of God, he would have thought himself. And his presence did the trick; seeing their Chancellor the students must have paused, and then most likely Thomas spoke, in a strong, calm voice, ordering them to put up their swords and return to their houses immediately. As Richard Strange put it, '... maintaining discipline with vigour, without slackening the reins to a noxious liberty.'

A more serious riot, one of the worst in Thomas's time, occurred in 1263 when the country was divided between those who backed Simon de Montfort's party and those loyal to the King. As soon as the Mayor of Oxford, a loyal Montfortian, heard that the King's eldest son, Prince Edward, was approaching the town, he closed the gates so that Edward was barred from marching in and the students from heading out to attack the Prince's retinue. At dinner time when the big bell of Saint Mary's was tolled, the students, furious at being imprisoned inside the town, collected their swords, halberds, slings and bows, and set about the townspeople, wreaking their revenge. They burned the Provost's Lodgings, they broke into William the espycer's house, wrecking his spicery and all his stock, and the Mayor, who was a vintner, fled at the sight of the invading horde who burst into his cellars, seizing and drinking his choicest wine, then sousing each other with the dregs.[10]

In the late eighteenth century the historian, Anthony Wood, wrote:

Mark the chronicles aright,
When Oxford students fall to fight
Before many months expired
England will with war be fired.[11]

If, following the riot of 1263, Thomas had heard this rhyme, he would surely have found it grimly prophetic.

CHAPTER III

As foretold in the chronicles war did follow the student riots of 1263. It was a war preceded by a sequence of events in which Thomas was increasingly involved for they focused on the cause of people's rights, a matter of the deepest concern to him.

One issue that gave rise to the discontent that led to war was Henry III's extravagance. Though, since Magna Carta, his tax-raising powers were limited, he spent lavishly and unrestrainedly. He spent on ceremonies: in one year alone there was the marriage of his sister to Emperor Frederick II, followed by his own to Eleanor of Provence, both magnificent affairs which cost enormous sums. He spent on building, his finest achievement being the new Abbey of Westminster which, with its multiple windows and pointed arches, was in graceful contrast to the massive and rounded Norman style. He spent on lands, on adding to his realm, acquiring Sicily, for instance, for his second son Edmund, at the cost of over one hundred and thirty-five thousand marks.[1]

Probably Henry's most unpopular extravagance

was the handout of gifts, titles and lands, to his foreign relations. Through his marriage he had acquired a large number of French in-laws most of whom he established in favoured positions. But though this was resented by his overtaxed subjects, far greater resentment, indeed positive loathing, was felt for his stepbrothers, the de Lusignans, the sons of his mother's second marriage, who came to England from France in the late 1240s and decided to stay. According to the chronicler, Matthew Paris,[2] the most hated of all the stepbrothers was Aymer de Lusignan, who, despite his scorn of all things English, was happy to accept Henry's offer of the bishopric of Winchester. Matthew Paris tells how Bishop Aymer persecuted the monks, how he threw a visiting official into prison and, more outrageous still, drugged his dinner guests in order to rob them. The fact that in the new abbey at Westminster the de Lusignan shields were among those carved on the walls of the arcades along the nave, shows how well they had infiltrated Henry's circle.

Another heavy drain on the royal purse was the constant demand for papal taxes which Henry, as an obedient Catholic, never thought to challenge, but could never meet.

Matters came to a head in 1258. People everywhere, at every level of society, had had enough of Henry's selfish government. In January Londoners gathered in the churchyard of Saint Paul's, the traditional meeting place for public protest, to voice their complaints. There were similar gatherings in other towns. As winter turned to spring Henry learned that he owed the Pope ninety thousand pounds; failure to pay off the debt in full would result in nothing less than excommunication.

It was impossible for Henry to raise additional tax without the consent of his most powerful barons. This he knew they were unlikely to give; he tried nonetheless. Among these barons was Simon de Montfort, the Earl of Leicester, who, ironically, was not only a Frenchman with an English title but was also Henry's brother-in-law, thus a candidate for public hatred on two counts.

Simon de Montfort had come to England as a young man to claim the earldom of Leicester, inherited through the marriage of his grandfather. With intelligence, ambition and considerable charm, he soon won Henry's friendship – they were close in age. But their friendship was stormy and Simon's secret marriage to Henry's sister, Eleanor, caused a major rift. It also made him the greatest landowner in England. A brilliant soldier, he campaigned in the Holy Land and later, on Henry's behalf, served as governor in Gascony for four years. His recall to England, which he bitterly resented, caused a further rift with Henry who owed him money, an enormous sum. It could be that his commitment to reform, first evident about this time, was sparked by his exasperation with Henry's extravagance and incompetent leadership. The single-minded vigour with which he pursued his campaign for change helped transform his public image from that of intruder to popular hero.

Henry's appeal spurred his barons into action. In April they rode to Westminster 'armed in excellent fashion and girded with swords' and demanded reform. Henry had no option; he agreed.

A council of twenty-four was set up composed of magnates (a term for the 'great men' of the realm who dealt with the king on the community's behalf), and senior churchmen. Twelve were chosen by the king, twelve by the opposition, among whom were Thomas's uncle, Walter Cantilupe and his cousin, Peter de Montfort. The council agreed to meet at Oxford in June to report their proposals to a parliament.[3] At the Oxford parliament in 1258 a detailed list of provisions was drawn up, the Provisions of Oxford as it came to be known, and, after much discussion, King Henry and the nineteen-year-old Prince Edward gave their assent 'for the correction and reform of their own affairs and of the state of the realm'.

First a new council of fifteen was elected, the Earl of Gloucester's brother, Hugh Bigod was appointed justiciar, the chief legal officer of the realm, there were also new sheriffs as well as custodians of major castles, all of whom were responsible to the council rather than the king. For the next four months a systematic enquiry was carried out into the administration of government and the law throughout the realm. Everything from the royal household to the local hundred courts came under careful scrutiny; the results, written down and authenticated with a seal, were submitted to the council in October. The outcome, the Provisions of Westminster, was approved by the parliament which met at Westminster the following Michaelmas.

The Provisions were made widely known and were generally welcomed for, other than the king, everyone stood to benefit. Certainly Thomas would have approved their aim; to transfer power from the king to the magnates, to those who represented the community. In fact the main feature of the reforms concerned the appointment of Henry's officials and ministers. This was now to be regulated by the council rather than the king alone. Hatred of the de Lusignans died hard. Yet there were changes in the administration of justice which, without doubt, improved the chance of a fair hearing for those at the bottom of the social scale. For the first time oral complaints in place of writs were acceptable in all courts rather than, as previously, in the king's courts only. This was a huge advantage for the vast majority who could not read or write. It could even be that Thomas, with his legal training, had influenced the adoption of this idea. He knew Simon de Montfort well, through his uncle, Walter Cantilupe, and through his cousin, Peter de Montfort, confusingly unrelated to Earl Simon. Added to that all three were neighbours in Warwickshire; the Cantilupe family seat at Aston Cantlow and Peter de Montfort's home as Beaudesert, were both close to Kenilworth, Simon de Montfort's main English base. Another link was that Simon, a zealous Catholic, was, like Thomas, a friend and follower of the great reforming bishop, Robert Grosseteste. Again, like Thomas, he believed in rooting out corruption in the church. Shady dealings such as simony, the trafficking in ecclesiastical preferment, and pluralism, the holding of several benefices, were widespread at that time.

So though not directly involved at this stage, Thomas must have watched with keen interest for signs that the reforms were progressing well. The signs were disappointing, certainly at first. The changes were too drastic, too suddenly imposed, there was so much detail, so much to go wrong. And, as the months went by and the initial impetus was lost, more and more problems came to light. A fundamental difficulty was that the administration was now under the joint control of the magnates and the king, a king consecrated to rule his subjects and who, as the head of the regime, was inseparable from his kingdom. An insoluble conundrum, the magnates found. Soon there were those, perhaps in the council, certainly among the less powerful barons, who began to doubt such a hybrid form of government would work at all. And when it became personal, when their own authority was undermined, a number of barons withdrew from their pledge to keep the Provisions. Matthew Paris [4] tells of a dispute between Simon de Montfort and his long-standing friend, Richard de Clare, Earl of Gloucester, a dispute almost certainly caused by the application of the 'wholesome statutes' set out in the Provisions to the Earl of Gloucester's lands, and one which resulted in such ill feeling that Earl Simon went storming off abroad.

At the end of 1259 Henry received another blow. Having already lost control of his household, many of his castles and, worst of all, control over the use of the royal seal, he now lost most of his Angevin empire. The Treaty of Paris, signed on 4th December after two years of negotiations with King Louis, bound Henry to renounce his claim to Normandy, Poitou, Angevin and Maine. Of his French lands only Gascony remained and that he held merely as a fief to the French crown.

Henry had had enough. A royal clerk, John Mansel, was despatched to Rome to have serious words, on the king's behalf, with Pope Alexander. Eventually, after long deliberation, the words bore fruit and a papal bull was issued absolving Henry from his oath to be bound by the Provisions. This triumph, as it must have seemed to Henry, given teeth by the decision of a board of arbitrators reinstating Henry's right to appoint sheriffs, was to accelerate Thomas's entry into politics.

Whether Thomas had ambitions in that direction is hard to tell. Observing how closely his uncle was involved in affairs of state, the idea must have occurred to him. After all many churchmen were appointed to positions in government, while a few, such as Thomas Becket, did it the other way about. At the time, however, May 1262, Thomas was absorbed in academic life. His role as Chancellor of Oxford was intensely demanding. The students were restless; at the least provocation fighting would break out, spreading, on occasion, into full-blown riots, difficult to quell.

Not only at Oxford. While Henry, his chosen legal officers in place, felt confident enough to be away in France, England grew increasingly turbulent. In towns and villages the people were divided against each other. There were those who resented the newly-acquired power of the barons and, in the towns, that of mayors and aldermen. Townsfolk marched through the streets, held protest meetings with militant speakers and proclamations. Through the winter of 1262–63, these disturbances multiplied and during the following summer Londoners again met at Saint Paul's. This time they were angry, so angry they attacked the great abbey at Westminster, forcing the monks to hand over their royal charter.

In an account in *The Chronicle of Mayors and Sheriffs of London*[5] compiled about this time, the writer, probably Alderman Arnold FitzThedmar, describes the sense of political instability which he claims was caused by the actions of the *minutus populus*, the little people, as he refers to the commoners, against those in authority with their, allegedly, failed promises of liberties. FitzThedmar adds that, having bound themselves by oath to keep the peace, the commoners set about plundering the Jews and money-lenders from Cahors.

Meanwhile there was trouble yet again along the Welsh Border. The death of the greatest of the Marcher lords, Richard de Clare, the Earl of Gloucester, in July 1262, had given the Welsh leader, Llwelyn, the opportunity to renew his attacks on the border castles. Many of these strongholds belonged to Prince Edward.

The Prince, who had until then backed the Provisions, came home from Gascony and changed his mind. He saw the ruin of his Border estates, witnessed in London at first hand the insulting of his mother by a hostile mob, more ominous still, he realized the threat to his own future as England's king. Now his full allegiance was to his father.

Simon de Montfort, also returning from abroad, rallied his followers, then together they demanded, yet again, that Henry keep to the Provisions, furthermore that he treat as enemies all those who opposed them. Unsurprisingly, Henry refused. Eventually, towards the end of the year, a compromise was reached; King Louis would act as arbitrator between the two sides.

In December 1263 the two delegations met King Louis at Amiens to present their case. Four commissioners represented the barons' party; Peter de Montfort, Humphrey de Bohun, the son of the Earl of Hereford, Simon de Montfort's son Henry – the Earl, with a broken leg, was forced to remain at Kenilworth – and, lastly, a man who was trusted by both kings as well as by Simon de Montfort, a nobleman of stature and experience, Thomas Cantilupe.

King Louis' judgement, the Mise of Amiens, was given on 23rd January 1264. It went against the barons on every count and ended with an injunction to both sides that they should renounce all rancour to each other. What hope of that? What hope of avoiding war?

The war began in the Welsh Marches, where Roger Mortimer was Simon de Montfort's most powerful enemy, then moved east across the Severn to Gloucester. In March Henry ordered his army to meet at Oxford. The masters and scholars were sent home for safety and, though Thomas was no longer Chancellor, he may have joined the party of bishops, one of them his uncle, Walter Cantilupe, who called on the king to try once more to reach a settlement. In a sense the many efforts of the churchmen to negotiate for peace strengthened Henry's hand for it showed up the divisions in the opposition, the churchmen urging a peaceful solution, the barons eager to fight it out. Certainly at that stage Henry was in no mood to talk. Peremptorily dismissed, the bishops retreated to the Friary church, where they excommunicated everyone opposed to the Provisions, which may have made them feel better, and the war went on.

The next confrontation was at Northampton where, on Passion Sunday, 7th April, Edward captured the castle, then the town, taking many prisoners, some of them leading Montfortians. In May the two armies met again, this time in Sussex, near the small town of Lewes. By then Simon's followers had dwindled further for a number of his younger barons, old friends of Prince Edward, had switched sides. Nonetheless, in a great show of support for the Provisions and for their hero, the Earl of Leicester, a great raggle-taggle army, people of all ranks, labourers, burghers, merchants, friars, as well as a crowd of

Londoners, travelled to Lewes to join the fight. As they waited in the woods for the battle to begin there must have been an air of crusade about it, the feeling that this was a holy war. On the eve of battle, out on the downs overlooking Lewes with its castle, priory, its cluster of dwellings, Earl Simon knighted a number of noblemen; one was Gilbert de Clare, the young Earl of Gloucester.

Early next morning – it was 14th April – absolved by Walter Cantilupe, they rode into battle wearing the cross of the crusades.

Within hours they were victorious. Among those taken prisoner were Prince Edward and the King. Later that day, with the dead still on the ground – there were over 600 foot soldiers killed, a virtual wipe-out of Londoners – a form of peace was drawn up and sealed with the seals of the King and Prince. Under the terms of the Mise of Lewes, as the complete settlement was named, Edward and his first cousin, Henry of Almain, became hostages to guarantee the terms were fulfilled, while certain Montfortian prisoners captured at Northampton were released. Three 'electors', Simon de Montfort, Gilbert de Clare, the young Earl of Gloucester, and Stephen Berkstead, Bishop of Chichester, would nominate a council of nine members.

One nominee was Thomas Cantilupe.

From now on Thomas was to play a more prominent role in government. At the same time his uncle, until then Simon de Montfort's closest adviser, was beginning to withdraw. That another bishop, Berkstead of Chichester, was one of the three 'electors' was proof that Walter Cantilupe was growing old.

In the Song of Lewes, a Latin poem written after the battle, probably by a Franciscan, Simon de Montfort is described as a faithful vassal entrusted to maintain co-operation, through a council, of king and community. The poet likens the realm to the human body, an organized unity, not, as the royalists saw it, an association of barons and freemen, each with independent rights, held together by a free and independent king. As expressed by the poet the authority of the community should be greater than that of the king alone, however wise he might be.

This, less lyrically expressed, was the gist of the Mise of Lewes. All officials from the justiciar downwards were to be chosen by the council of nine; in the case of disagreement a two-thirds majority should decide. The three 'electors' had the final say. Thus power was far more closely concentrated than in the government of 1258. Even so Simon de Montfort had no delusions about the stability of his position. As an immediate precaution against local rebellion, 'a keeper of the peace' was to be appointed in every county, a type of chief constable, who would oversee the maintenance of law and order.

As it happened, however, the immediate threat came not from within England but from northern France, where a band of royalist exiles was preparing to invade. Rallied by the feisty Queen Eleanor, at her best in a crisis, they had collected troops, weapons, ships. The danger was real and imminent.

At once the council acted; every county was ordered to gather quotas of men who, under the command of a local officer, would be ready to act, to defend their land from a 'great host of aliens', as the exiles were described by a Saint Alban's chronicler (not Matthew Paris, who had died in 1259). It must have been heartening for Earl Simon that so many were prepared to take up arms against the royalists and, throughout the summer while the harvest over-ripened in the fields, to remain on guard.

At the same time the council took steps to settle matters peacefully. They renewed negotiations with the royalists on both sides of the Channel, not hesitating to use their strongest card, the fate of their two royal prisoners. Should King Louis, naturally in league with the royalists, encourage an invasion, the lives of his kinsmen, Henry and Edward, could not be guaranteed. This warning was repeated several times; there could have been no doubt.

The negotiations dragged on, and on. The Pope intervened on behalf of the King stating that Earl Simon, 'the pestilent man', should be 'plucked out of the realm of England' and an order was issued for his excommunication. It was not until March 1265 that the terms of settlement were finally agreed. These involved the exchange of castles and lands, and of a number of prisoners, among them Roger Mortimer who was to go to Ireland for a year and a day with two of the other Marcher lords. All parts of the realm including Gascony were covered by the terms; they were detailed, comprehensive, and they were intended to last.

A proclamation setting out the 'rule of the kingdom' which, on the orders of the council, was to be read aloud in every county court at least once a year, ended with the statement that both the King and Prince Edward had sworn on oath to maintain the peace and observe the charters of liberties. And should either fail to do so, Henry added in his public declaration, 'which Heaven forbid', everyone must work to do them harm.

Fine words. Yet, though they came from the man who was his captive, how confident did Simon feel?

News reached him of disputes among his younger followers, disputes that grew increasingly bitter, that stemmed for the most part from rivalries among the friends of his sons. One of those involved was his leading supporter, Gilbert de Clare.

Meanwhile he had appointed a new Chancellor.

In fact it was the council of nine who chose the Chancellor. Most likely in this instance their choice and Simon's coincided. The Chancellor of England was, in a sense, a go-between, the link between the council and the king. The Chancellor had control of all public documents; he was also responsible for the writing and sealing of every royal letter. Plainly, therefore, his own politics mattered a good deal. The outgoing Chancellor, John of Chishill, who had been chosen by the King before the battle of Lewes, had shown little commitment to the Provisions. He was replaced by a trusted Montfortian.

On 25th February 1265 Thomas Cantilupe, Chancellor of England, came centre stage.

CHAPTER IV

In his biography of Thomas, Richard Strange describes how, according to custom, when Thomas first took on the Chancellorship the King hung the great seal round his neck. There were three seals, one gold and two silver, large and small. Strange also tells us that, as Chancellor, Thomas 'showed great wisdom and integrity'. Which comes as no surprise; it was for these qualities he was chosen for this key position at what was undoubtedly a tricky and unstable time. It was also an exceedingly busy time for an enormous backlog of business had built up during the recent disturbances. There was the documentation concerning the transference of lands and castles to new ownership, the aim being to keep strategic areas in Montfortian hands; there was the normally flourishing wool trade with Flanders which, having lapsed during the war, had to be reopened; there were the exiles to be summoned to return to England. Among them was the Queen's uncle, Archbishop Boniface of Canterbury, a native of Savoy, who, as Matthew Paris wrote 'was noted more for his birth than his brains' and who had left for France in 1263 to raise support for the King. Another Savoyard due to be recalled was Peter Aquablanca, the unpopular Bishop of Hereford. Thomas's in-tray, his 'hanaper' – a hamper in which waiting documents were kept – must have been extremely full.

Thomas worked in his own department where, under his supervision, the chancery clerks, both senior and junior, enscribed letters or writs with fine quill pens on parchment. (Parchment, the treated skins of young animals, generally kid or calf, was the medieval alternative to paper which was not readily available in England until the fourteenth century.)

As well as matters resulting from the recent upheavals, there were the more general issues; building works, for instance, land grants, appointments, scutage (money paid in lieu of service), clerical taxes, boundaries and that was not all. Every letter was recorded on the appropriate chancery roll, a parchment document often many yards long, stored in the chancery under the direction of the senior clerk, the master of the rolls. There were a number of rolls each dealing with a department; close rolls, for example, recorded letters 'usually of an executive nature' concerning a wide range of issues from writs to summon parliament to the accounts of the royal household. Patent rolls recorded writs concerning matters such as licences, proclamations, royal grants; charter rolls the documents dealing with the ownership of land. And so on, and so on.

To take on the office of Chancellor, to face such a mountain of detail, notwithstanding the back-up of experienced clerks, must have been daunting to say the least. Or perhaps it was a challenge; Thomas would most likely have seen it so. From the five rolls that survive from his time in office it is clear that he got to grips with his new post immediately, that he tackled it with vigour, and with thoroughness. There was no skating over the surface of things, of sealing letters as instructed by the King without delving into the rights and wrongs of each particular case. Earlier Chancellors had been criticized for failing to follow the terms of the Provisions. No such charge could be levelled at Thomas. As set out in the settlement of 1264 the King was to manage the affairs of the realm on the advice of the council of nine. As Chancellor, Thomas was chief of the council, the opposition in Henry's eyes. Yet Henry had accepted his appointment willingly, 'garanter' as the record states. Relations between them were clearly good. Thomas treated Henry's instructions with respect. That Henry was the King, and by divine right, was something Thomas could not dismiss and it may be that the position of the King as a figurehead devoid of power, worried him increasingly. Nonetheless Thomas kept an independent mind; he was nobody's poodle, neither Henry's nor the council's, and there is evidence that in certain cases he refused to seal a writ or letter. William Cantilupe, a nephew of Thomas and his clerk at one time, tells of Thomas returning his seal to the King because he felt a particular letter should not be dispatched. Apparently, if this story is true, Henry acceded to Thomas's view and returned the seal. On another occasion Thomas refused to seal a letter that had been authorized by four prominent members of the council of nine. The letter, to the citizens of Lincoln, concerned the toll paid at the Boston fair, one of the great wool fairs and a major trading event. The patent rolls for 7th March 1265, recorded that ... *cancellarius non consentit illu litterae*; '... the Chancellor did not consent to that letter.'

Another issue where Thomas showed characteristic independence of mind was over the acceptance of gifts. The Provisions of Oxford, the settlement of 1264, required officials to swear they would take no reward. Richard Swinfield, who followed Thomas as Bishop of Hereford, happened to be present when a party of monks, who were visiting the King, offered Chancellor Thomas a valuable jewel. Courteously Thomas refused; he also reminded the monks that they were wrong to offer him a present; they must think him 'pliable and corruptible'. As if anyone could think that of Thomas. So it may seem strange, on the face of it at least, that Thomas negotiated an increase in the Chancellor's salary. In fact, as set out clearly in the Provisions of Oxford, the King was to pay his 'servants sufficiently so that they have no need to accept anything from anyone else'. Thomas reasoned that the Chancellor's salary, which from 1261 had been fixed at four hundred marks a year, was inadequate; indeed 'rewards' to supplement insufficient pay could even be seen as a necessity. Thomas's reasoning was effective; on 26th March Henry instructed that a writ should be made out granting Thomas five hundred marks annually for the upkeep of his staff and himself. It is recorded on the current Liberate roll that Henry, with various ministers, witnessed the sealing of the writ which he then folded with his own hand. As this was the only occasion throughout his reign when he made such a gesture, which perhaps he did with something of a flourish, it was seen to be of great significance. It certainly confirmed, beyond all doubt, that Thomas had not raised his own salary.[1]

Another indication of Thomas's responsible approach to his role as Chancellor revealed in the chancery rolls, is the marked increase in the number of letters that were authorized. The close roll for the four months before his appointment show that out of some two hundred letters only twenty-three were authorized. While he was in office one hundred and eight of the one hundred and seventy letters issued were authorized. Plainly he judged it important to make known on whose orders a letter had been issued. And it may well be that he felt so all the more during the current uncertainty.

Daily it grew more ominous; the instability throughout the land. It was a feeling that hung in the air, an undercurrent of violence waiting to surface, to flare up and spread into further war. In his long rhyming history, recounting events from Roman Britain to the Barons' War, the chronicler, Robert of Gloucester, who unusually writes in English, gives a powerful sense of the rising tension at that time.

Back in February the young Earl of Derby, Robert de Ferrers, one of Simon's leading supporters, had been imprisoned in the Tower for wilful trespasses – on Simon's orders. Outraged, Robert's friends deserted Simon; there had already been defections. The most serious was yet to come. Simon, aware of the increasingly bitter feud between his sons and his leading supporter, the twenty-year-old Gilbert de Clare, must have feared the outcome. For some time Gilbert, who, as one of the three electors should have been right at the hub of decision making, had kept himself apart, found excuses to stay away from court. In early May the court moved to Gloucester. It was quite usual for the court to move from place to place, the entire court, which of course included the Chancellor. But yet again there was no Gilbert de Clare. Robert of Gloucester tells how the young Earl camped on a hill overlooking the town; at night he lit fires which glowed like warning points across the countryside. There he was close by, yet out of sight. 'When one thought he was far, oft he was near.' He sent messages to Simon, objecting to the treatment of the King, to the exaltation of Simon's sons. Fact or fiction, it paints a vivid picture. Fact certainly was the news that Gilbert was meeting Roger Mortimer, Simon's most powerful enemy. Instead of going to Ireland for a year and a day, as agreed in the Mise of Lewes, Roger Mortimer and his fellow Marcher barons had stayed at home, stirring trouble in the borderlands.

Walter Cantilupe, now old and frail, tried yet again to save the situation. With the Justiciar and other magnates he arranged for Gilbert to meet Simon at Gloucester in early May. The meeting never took place.

It was at that moment, on 7th May, that Thomas left the court. He handed the seal to Ralph of Sandwich, the keeper of the royal wardrobe (the king's treasury), and went to London.

Why? It was in fact not unusual for the Chancellor to be absent from time to time. Besides Thomas had made arrangements to cover his absence, meticulous arrangements, leaving nothing to chance. Ralph of Sandwich, who would keep the seal in the king's wardrobe, would seal only routine writs, others must be sealed with the consent of one of three principal members of the council. So Thomas did not leave unexpectedly.

Did he mean to return?

It has been suggested by Sir Maurice Powicke[2] that

Thomas had 'been advised' to leave, that some members of the council found Thomas too apt to question their advice, to follow his own judgement in sealing letters, as he had over the Boston fair. Perhaps he was, in their opinion, too independent, too dogmatic. They had to be sure how he would use the seal; uncertainty at such a critical time simply would not do. Had they come out with it, made their feelings plain, would Thomas have resigned? Probably, after careful thought, he would, with admirable calm and dignity. There is no evidence to suggest he did resign. In fact a royal letter was authorized by Thomas, in co-operation with Peter de Montfort and Hugh Despencer, the Justiciar, on 7th May, the very day he left. Then again at the end of May when the court had moved to Hereford a letter referring to 'master Thomas Cantilupe our Chancellor'[3] was sent for his attention 'if he is still staying in London', which suggests he was expected to return to court.

It may well be that his leaving had more to do with personal doubts. The historian T. F. Tout, whose comprehensive research delved deep into thirteenth-century politics, believed Thomas may have been 'weakening in his support of revolutionary government'.

It is not hard to imagine Thomas agonizing over loyalty, spending hours on his knees praying for guidance. He was Chancellor, he was chief of the council, a trusted and true Montfortian. And yet, and yet, Henry was King, his right to be so was divine, he was Thomas's friend, as was Edward, his heir. They trusted Thomas, had faith in him. What should he do?

It would be strange if Thomas had not consulted his uncle. Walter Cantilupe was certainly at Gloucester then, getting nowhere in attempting to reconcile

Simon with Gilbert de Clare. Knowing Thomas so well, he was bound to have noticed his nephew was troubled. And had Thomas remained silent, not wanting to burden the old man, Walter would surely have questioned him. And had they talked, deeply, late into the night, Walter may have hinted, given the impression, if not said outright, that he shared Thomas's doubts.

Speculation, no more. Yet if it is true that, as he lay dying in February of the following year, Walter Cantilupe confessed he had been wrong in supporting the baronial cause, then the story is more believable.[4]

Another possible clue to why Thomas left Gloucester may be found in a badly damaged letter sent to Henry from London signed 'Cantilup'. The letter, mainly concerning a request made to the Dean and Chapter of Saint Paul's, also mentions messengers from the King of France, who 'in a short time are about to come to England'. It is known that Earl Simon did expect messengers from King Louis at that time; it could be, therefore, that Thomas had gone south in order to meet them and return with them to court. Records show that on 26th May an emissary from France did arrive. But if Thomas did meet him and set out with him for Gloucester they would not have got far.

By late May the political situation had grown more volatile, more dangerous. The court had moved to Hereford, closer to the Marches where Roger Mortimer with his fellow barons were a major threat.

At that stage Simon seems to have believed he could still count on Gilbert de Clare for he had given the duty of guarding the captive Prince Edward at Hereford to his younger brother, Thomas de Clare.

On 28th May, Thomas de Clare rode out with Edward for exercise. Suddenly together they broke away from the other guards and galloped at top speed to Wigmore castle, the home of Roger Mortimer. From there they sped on to Ludlow where they were joined by Roger Mortimer. They were also joined by Gilbert de Clare.

Gilbert's involvement in Edward's escape, his duplicity, must have been for Simon a most bitter blow. He decided to approach Llywelyn of Wales to negotiate a peace, thereby adding to his military strength. The bargaining was tough, long drawn-out. Eventually, in exchange for peace, hedged about with conditions, the wily Welshman gained recognition as well as considerable lands; Simon got a force of Welsh infantry.

For the next five weeks, like players in a chess game, checking, outwitting, the protagonists moved their knights and soldiers about the Midlands, criss-crossed the Severn, met at Evesham. There, early on 4th August, Edward attacked, closing in from the north. Roger Mortimer blocked the way across the Avon. Simon, with the King, was cut off in the middle of the town. They fought ferociously, Simon and his men, forming a circle around the King, but at the end it was Edward's victory.

Henry wounded, cried, 'Slay me not! I am Henry of Winchester!' and was rescued from the slaughter. Which was indiscriminate and terrible.

One corpse, dragged triumphantly to open ground, was decapitated, its genitals were then cut off. As the butchery was done, it was said that the sky grew strangely dark.

A portent? A second coming, even? This was the corpse of no ordinary man.

As Robert of Gloucester comments '... it was most pitifully done that Sir Simon the old man was dismembered so ...'[5]

Afterwards Simon de Montfort's head, with the testicles dangling either side of the nose, was taken to Wigmore. '... To Dame Maude the Mortimer they sent it most foully ... This saw Robert ... and was soreafeared'.

The body was buried by the monks of Evesham, it is hoped with compassion and dignity. Among his followers and friends, and these included Thomas, Simon's memory was greatly honoured and belief in his holiness was strong. It was said that Thomas's steward, and his hawk, were cured of illness by Simon's intervention. Certainly soon after his death pilgrims travelled to his grave, stories of his miracles were told, ballads sung of the great Earl Simon '... martyred for the justice of the land and for truth'.

CHAPTER V

The news of Evesham when it reached Thomas in London must have hit hard, stirring confusion in his mind, and in his heart; sadness at so many killed; Earl Simon, Hugh Despenser, and his kinsman Peter de Montfort, the list went on and on – mixed with thankfulness that the King and Prince Edward were both safe. At the same time he must have felt uneasiness about his own situation, even perhaps a touch of fear. He was, after all, one of the leading Montfortians, the chief of the council, the Chancellor. Though he had handed the seal to Ralph of Sandwich, he had not resigned. How would he be treated by the new regime?

Obviously any hopes he may have had of resuming as Chancellor were entirely dead. And, though he had been on reasonably good terms with Henry, there had been disagreements; he had stood out against Henry more than once.

For a time he kept his head down, probably in London, for the King was away recovering from his wounds, first at Gloucester and later at Marlborough.

Meanwhile at Kenilworth young Simon de Montfort was holding out against the royalist siege, while some areas in the south, Essex and the Weald of Kent, were still in rebel hands. It was as these last pockets of resistance were being dealt with by military means that Ottobuono Fieschi arrived in England. This distinguished cardinal had been sent by Pope Clement to 'reintegrate the state of the realm'. To deal justly with the Montfortian barons and clergy, to sort out the return of lands and goods plundered in the war, then to draw up a lasting settlement, was a daunting challenge for anyone.[1] But Ottobuono, who as papal legate wielded considerable power, was a shrewd and experienced intermediary and eventually, after long consultation, terms were agreed. The Dictum of Kenilworth, as it was known, was published at Kenilworth on 31st October 1266, '... in the name of the Holy and undivided Trinity ... for the good, prosperous and peaceable state of King Henry'. It stated that the King should rule through reliable men, respect the freedom of the church and his subjects; it also dealt fairly with the rebels, offering them terms that allowed them to redeem their lands by buying them back at a rate that depended on their level of guilt.

In the meantime, long before Ottobuono had worked out the Dictum, Thomas had heard reassuring news. It was, in fact, soon after Evesham that he received letters granting him safe conduct to go anywhere in England that he wished. This must have been a great relief to him for it showed that, though out of favour politically, he was not altogether *persona non grata* in Henry's eyes.[2]

It also meant he could visit his livings. How safe it was to travel round the country with scattered rebels still at large in the forests was debatable, but Thomas was never known to be deterred by danger. The church was what mattered; it mattered to Thomas above all else and, as he can have had little time to attend to his livings in the past few months, that would have been his first intention. He had by this time acquired a good many. Several had come to him through family connections, among them Aston-Cantlow in Warwickshire, Bradwell in Essex, Bulwick in Northamptonshire, Wintringham and Deighton in Yorkshire, the last a gift from the splendidly named Dame Agatha Trussebut. Besides these he held three livings in Worcestershire and a handful along the south Wales border. One appointment which meant a great deal to him was the canonry of Saint Paul's granted to him in 1246, while he was a student at Orleans. In later life when he spent much of his time in London he often took part in the services at Saint Paul's, preaching such fine sermons and attending Mass so regularly that this was mentioned in the evidence of the canonization process. When he became Bishop of Hereford, he may sometimes have made use of a house in Old Fish Street Hill belonging to the Hereford diocese.[3] It was while he was staying in London that Brother Martin, then the sacristan at Saint Bartholomew's, came to know Thomas and who, at the canonization hearings, gave a description of Thomas's appearance. Thanks solely to Brother Martin we know that Thomas was a redhead though by then, in middle age, his hair and beard were streaked with white, and that he had a long nose and a fresh complexion.

Thomas was granted at least two more livings in 1265, the year of Evesham, when he became not only Rector of Coleby in Lincolnshire, but also, more importantly, Archdeacon of Stafford, a position which brought with it a canonry of Lichfield cathedral.

And with further livings to be added in the future, it is clear that altogether Thomas made good use of the dispensation given him by Pope Innocent IV in 1245 to hold livings in plurality.

Yet he was criticized for doing so, accused of being a pluralist, of procuring livings for financial gain while neglecting his parishioners. Though in Thomas's case this was far from true, it happened so often that pluralism had gained a bad name. There were some senior churchmen, Walter Cantilupe for one, who actually spoke out in its favour maintaining that priests of noble birth needed the income from several livings to keep up a suitable lifestyle, to entertain and to give to charity. It was the upper class priests who were the worst offenders. Land equalled money and power; certain livings covered valuable land. A nobleman, therefore, would use his influence to procure the best livings for a younger son, sometimes doing so long before the boy was old enough to be ordained, in which case a deputy would be installed and paid a minimal wage, while the father pocketed the difference. One of the most notorious pluralists was Bogo de Clare, a son of the Earl of Gloucester, who by the end of his life – he died in 1291 – held twenty-four livings and a number of canonries. He seldom went near any of them though they brought him in an income of two thousand two hundred pounds, roughly a million and a quarter in today's money. Not enough for Bogo, who spent so much on luxury foods, sweetmeats and imported spices, particularly preserved ginger, that he ran up colossal debts.[4]

Thomas was the antithesis of Bogo. He was

immensely conscientious, taking great care to find for each of his livings a deputy priest known to be of good moral character and who would carry out his duties properly. As many clergy at that time had little education and doubtful morals this was not as easy as it sounds. Thomas kept a watchful eye on them, travelling long distances, often through remote and densely wooded countryside, to visit each parish. He would stay for several days meeting the parishioners, calling on the sick and elderly, bringing them presents, chiefly food: corn, beans and pease (dried peas for pease pudding), also fuel and warm clothing. Between visits he would arrange with local bailiffs for food and fuel to be distributed to those in need. He would also provide funds for repairs to buildings and, whenever on his travels he came to a bridge he judged unsafe, he would pay in advance for repair work to be done. Which sounds naively trusting, but Thomas, with his legal mind, would surely have checked later to make sure the work had been carried out.

And, if his critics argued that charity is easy for a man of means and that Thomas, with his great inherited wealth, had no need to top it up with the income from so many livings, he would have told them firmly that the Church had a duty to exact its due, a view widely held in medieval times. He would have also pointed out that a person should receive the rate for the job, adding that each of his deputies was paid according to the value of the living.

A large proportion of a priest's income came from tithe, a form of tax compulsory since the eighth century.[5] Tithe was levied on produce of all kinds from corn to garden herbs and on all stock, their young and their natural products; wool, eggs, beeswax, swansdown. Those who earned their living by their labours, tradesmen and artisans, for example, paid a tenth of their income in tithe with no allowance for expenses. Strict rules were laid down by the church and defaulters were severely punished. A kind-hearted bishop would sometimes spare the poorest from paying their tithe and, though there is no record that Thomas did so, at a guess, he did. Known for his strict enforcement of the rules, he was also known for his charity.

The following year brought Thomas both good and bad news. On 10th February as 'sometime Chancellor' a writ was issued admitting him to grace and forgiving him the King's 'rancour and indignation'. One other member of the council of nine, Giles de Argentan, who had been captured at Evesham, was also admitted to grace and forgiveness.

Next day Walter Cantilupe died. It would be good to think that Thomas was there, that, having received word of his royal forgiveness, he was able to pass on this news to the old man, who at the end of his life is said to have felt that he had been wrong in acting against the King. Had he known that Thomas who had stood for the same cause, had been restored to favour, he would surely have felt comforted. Unfortunately there is no record of Thomas's whereabouts then, nor when the news reached him, both good and bad. Communication was slow at any time; February weather could bring it to a halt for several weeks.

Walter Cantilupe was buried in Worcester Cathedral. His memorial is in the Lady Chapel in front of the altar. He was Simon de Montfort's oldest friend; he was much loved. Thomas, perhaps, loved him most of all.

At some time in 1267 Thomas learned that he had been fully accepted back into royal favour. He was named as 'king's clerk', an honorary title which did not include any involvement in Henry's government. There is no evidence that Thomas would have agreed to be involved in any case. Whatever his doubts about Henry's treatment during the last regime, his belief in the reforms was as strong as ever. Even so Henry wanted to make clear that Thomas was his personal friend. And surely Thomas must have assured the King that it was mutual.

However genuine his friendship with Henry it remained at arm's length. Perhaps Thomas decided it was better that way and therefore arranged to go abroad. Perhaps he was invited to return to his old university. Either way sometime in 1267 he travelled to Paris and found himself a place to live. He took lodgings in one of the narrow streets close to the university. Alongside the lecture halls and student lodgings were taverns and brothels where prostitutes were readily available at any time of day. Thomas must have been aware of what was going on around him however hard he tried to ignore it. Perhaps it was this, his apparent detachment, that brought him to the notice of Eadmund de Aimar, a friar preacher, who lived directly opposite. Later Eadmund related a story about Thomas, an intriguing and revealing story, which must have taken place soon after he arrived in Paris. How Eadmund heard the story is unknown but it is detailed and believable, it has, as the historian, Barbara Ross, puts it, the ring of truth. And why should Eadmund have invented it?

One day Thomas went with friends to change his English money at a burgher's house outside the city. They arrived late – perhaps they had trouble finding the house – and realized that the city gates would be closed before they returned. The money-changer's wife, a strikingly beautiful woman, offered Thomas a room for the night. His friends urged him to accept. Perhaps they stayed elsewhere or slept on the floor while Thomas, probably the most senior, and the one the woman had invited, occupied the room. It was a pleasant room with a comfortable bed; in one corner, unknown to Thomas, was a secret door. He woke in the night to feel someone climbing into bed and lying close to him. He edged away till he rolled onto the floor. Soon he heard the intruder creep from the room. In the morning the burgher's wife asked him how he had slept. Very badly, he replied, for he had been tempted by the Devil. The woman eyed him for a moment, then she asked him if he had been awake. She went on to say that if he told her truly she would answer truly in return. When Thomas told her that he had been awake she confessed that she had been the Devil, but from now on she promised to live a virtuous life.

Whether Thomas ever went back to find out if the burgher's wife had kept her promise – it was said that she had – seems unlikely. Women, all women, but emphatically one who he admitted had tempted him, were to be avoided in Thomas's view. No female servants, however old, were engaged in his household. No women, even his sisters, ever stayed overnight under his roof. Neither did any women testify at the canonization hearing, apart from those who spoke about his miracles.

In any case Thomas had come to Paris to absorb himself in theology. He must have looked forward to a period of peaceful study. In fact it must have turned out to be far from peaceful for each time he emerged from his rooms he would have found his fellow students arguing. The theology faculty was in turmoil, seething with conflicting views, views that ignited fierce debate, that spread throughout the university, through Paris itself. The cause of such commotion was nothing less than the human soul, its true definition. The traditional belief, inspired by Augustine and accepted by the church held that the soul was a separate entity; it existed on its own. This had recently been challenged by Thomas Aquinas, who though at that time was teaching at Viterbo, was soon to come to Paris as Master of Theology. Aquinas believed that the soul was part of the human being; it was integral to the complete individual. He did not put this forward as a suggestion; he had worked it out. It could be said that his conclusion was empirical. Based on Aristotelian philosophies he had written several comprehensive tomes proving it was true; his teaching is now part of official Catholic teaching. For such an esoteric question to set Paris on fire, verbally at least, may seem far-fetched, yet that is how it was. Many theologians strongly condemned Aquinas's works, among them the Dominican Robert Kilwardby, and his successor as Archbishop of Canterbury, the Franciscan, John Pecham. The Franciscans were forbidden to read them at all. Where did Thomas stand in this debate? He left no written work, no notes, no texts, and, though we know he lectured while in Paris, according to his Dominican friend, Edmund de Amauri, he stuck to the texts of the Epistles and Apocalypse, setting them out and explaining them without raising controversial questions.

It was while he was in Paris, probably in 1270, that a famous confrontation took place which may well have had a bearing on Thomas's future. It happened at an inception ceremony (the awarding of a master's degree) at the university where probably the most distinguished person present was Thomas Aquinas. During the proceedings an English Franciscan, John Pecham, spoke at length on a particular theory concerning the eternity of the world, which directly opposed Aquinas's view. Pecham may have done so deliberately for when Aquinas challenged him, he repeated his controversial speech. Aquinas rose again. There was perhaps a pause, an expectant hush before his words rang out, words so powerful, so devastatingly effective that Pecham cringed; he pleaded for enlightenment, he humbly begged. In front of such a gathering he looked a fool.

If Thomas was there, and most likely he was, that image of Pecham would have stuck, would have coloured his opinion of the man, diminished his respect. Possibly Pecham was aware of that. It cannot have helped their relationship in the time ahead.

CHAPTER VI

t last in 1272 Thomas went home, back once more to Oxford for the final stage of his theology studies. He must have felt it right to return, so that, as with his canon law studies twelve years earlier, he would receive his doctorate in his academic home, which Oxford surely must have been to him.

England had changed while he had been away. He had left disruption and bitterness, the aftermath of war; the Dictum of Kenilworth, the settlement engineered by Cardinal Ottobuono had not had time to take effect. Six years later the country was united, there was peace. Ottobuono had even masterminded a treaty with Llywelyn of Wales.

Another significant development had taken place soon after Thomas left for Paris; it was one that must have pleased him. The Provisions made at Westminster eight years before had been re-enacted. Above all this proved that, though the royalists had won the war, the Montfortian cause had not been lost. It had been at Marlborough, in November 1267, that Henry, Ottobuono and a gathering 'of the more discerning men of high and low estate', agreed to reissue the Provisions of Westminster in a full, detailed and permanent form. The statute of Marlborough set out once more the principles of the Great Charter of 1225, underlining their importance to people's lives, sending a message around the shires, setting them in stone.

In his final years Henry muddled along, his backlog of debt worsened by the war. In desperation to pay for 'necessities' he pawned 'a great and precious gold crown', jewels and other regalia, but as this was no more than a temporary measure, the huge debt remained. Once again it was Ottobuono who provided at least a partial solution. He had come to England for more than one reason; his brief from Pope Clement IV was, first, to provide a political settlement, second, and to Rome of more importance, to fire men with zeal to take up the cross, to go on crusade.[1] Ottobuono succeeded in doing so by the means of travelling friars recruited to preach, to spread the word. The idea of crusade grew popular; it became the fashion to take up the cross, or at any rate talk about doing so. More importantly it served as a focus, the country united, looked ahead, let go of the past.

Henry would lead the crusade; that was the plan. With him would go his sons, Edward and Edmund, his nephew, Henry of Almain, the Earl of Gloucester and many more. The drawback was the cost. Ottobuono dealt with that by levying a tax and, as owing to the disturbances, the clergy had paid no papal taxes for nearly ten years, he targeted them. Of course they protested at paying a twentieth of their income to the crown but eventually the tax raised close on fifty thousand pounds and, in July 1268, Ottobuono, harshly criticized for his efforts – no papal legate was ever popular – finally went home.

The following summer the crusaders set sail for the Holy Land. When it came to the point Henry decided not to go. He had not been well and for a man of sixty-three such a strenuous expedition would be unwise. Besides there was the risk of both he and Edward leaving the realm, perhaps for a considerable time. For much the same reason the Earl of Gloucester also changed his mind. Despite Llywelyn's truce, the Earl's marcher lands were vulnerable to attack from Welsh rebels. He was also said to be dissatisfied with the financial terms of the crusade.

Edward arrived at Carthage in Tunisia to learn that King Louis of France had died there of plague two months earlier. Now he must lead the crusade.

Having battled in Syria against the Egyptian infidels, probably without achieving very much, Edward moved his army to Acre where he was attacked by a muslim warrior, a genuine Assassin. His life was saved by his wife, Eleanor, who courageously sucked the venom from his wound. Soon afterwards she gave birth to their daughter, Joan 'of Acre'.

On 16th November 1272, Henry died at Westminster. Four days later the funeral took place in Henry's great new abbey, which had been dedicated three years before on the feast day of Edward the Confessor, the founder of the abbey and Henry's patron saint. It is likely that Thomas, newly-arrived from France, was among the great throng who attended the service; the churchmen, magnates, knights, Londoners. Immediately afterwards everyone present went to the high altar and, there and then, swore an oath of fealty to Edward, their new King. One of the first to take the oath was the Earl of

Gloucester, who had promised Henry on the day he died that he would guard the realm till the King returned.

For Edward was then in Sicily. He did not hurry home; he had no need, for the country was united behind him. He was already well known as a strong, trustworthy and Christian King. He was a well-built man, athletic and quick-witted with a forthright manner and a fiery temper. The unreliability he had shown when young, mainly in defiance of his father, was in the past; now, at thirty-three, he was authoritative and confident. Before he left England he had made sure the governing council consisted of those he could rely on entirely. His new Chancellor was the ecclesiastic magnate, Walter de Merton. His Archbishop of Canterbury, an appointment that became known a few days after the funeral, was the leader of the English Dominicans, Robert Kilwardby.

The following June Kilwardby travelled all the way from Canterbury to preside over Thomas's inception as a Doctor of Theology at the church of the Dominicans in Oxford, where until recently he had been the prior. It must have been for them both a very special occasion, memorable and moving. Though Kilwardby was senior to Thomas they had been friends since their first meeting forty-four years earlier when Kilwardby was tutor to Thomas at Oxford. Later they were together in Paris and possibly at Orleans for it was while Thomas was there, studying under Master Guido, that another student, who was later Kilwardby's auditor, had dreamed vividly, and as it turned out, prophetically, of Thomas wearing a mitre and sitting in Master Guido's chair.[2]

Kilwardby, who had achieved a distinguished university career before he became a Dominican, was the first of the order to lecture at Oxford. Addressing the gathering at the inception ceremony, he described Thomas as 'unspotted from the world' adding that he had 'never perceived him guilty of any mortal sin'.[3]

Kilwardby meant it. He was Thomas's confessor; he understood his motivations, his inner feelings, probably better than anyone.

Though Edward was still abroad – he spent eighteen months in Gascony before he returned – it is likely that by now he had been in touch with Thomas. They had known each other for many years and, despite Thomas's political views, Edward counted him as a reliable friend and one of impressive ability. Early in his reign, possibly before he returned to England, he chose Thomas as one of his councillors. To have Thomas at his councils and parliaments, giving his opinion, wise, unbiased, to have him at hand for one to one advice, Edward could see this would be invaluable. It was also on Edward's instructions that, in the spring or summer of 1273, Thomas received news of an important appointment. He was to be Chancellor of Oxford for a second term.

As far as is known he took up the post at the start of the Michaelmas term in 1273. As Regent of Theology he would have continued with some teaching, but the administrative work of the Chancellor was time-consuming and, more than ever, it demanded his diplomatic skill. For the university had grown in the last ten years, more students came from outlying areas, from Wales, northern England, even from Scotland, and as Thomas knew from past experience, it was the presence of these uncouth 'foreigners' – they were judged uncouth by those from the south and probably were – that stirred up trouble. The most serious confrontation during Thomas's second chancellorship happened in January 1274. As in 1262 southerners confronted northerners; again Thomas intervened thrusting his way into the middle of the fray, again his cloak was slashed, according to the records, by a northerner. The close rolls for that year record that following the riot Thomas, with Ralph de Hengam and others, was to act as a judge of the brawling students.

Soon afterwards he left Oxford and, with his nephew, William Cantilupe, travelled to France for an international gathering of churchmen. The second Council of Lyons was convened by the new Pope, Gregory X, with the aim of ending the division between the Greek and Latin churches. Gregory X, a man of courage and stature, took a wide-ranging view of the European political scene. He saw the danger of the vacuum left by the death of King Louis being filled by the powerful new Byzantine Emperor. The two churches should unite, join forces to defeat the infidel. As an ardent supporter of crusades – he had recently been in Acre with his friend, Prince Edward – he preached fervently at Lyons, urging the reconquest of Jerusalem, captured by Khwarazmian Turks thirty years before.

A crowd of high-powered churchmen attended the Council including the Franciscan, Saint Bonaventura. Another saint-to-be, Thomas Aquinas, died on his way there, which as he held opposing views to Bonaventura, must have spared the other delegates hours of arcane debate. Not that the Council was short of time. It lasted from 7th May to 17th July, ten weeks of earnest discussion on international matters as well as on church reform; ten weeks of good living, of processions and splendid pageantry, of wining and dining lavishly.

Not Thomas however, feasting was not his style. He appreciated fine food and wine and was renowned as a generous host. When in London he gave banquets for the great and good and later that year he gave a particularly sumptuous feast in honour of King Edward, who had at last come home. But Thomas always ate sparingly, diluting his wine with water; on principle he denied himself. Towards the end of his life he confided in a fellow priest that for thirty-two years he had not left the table after a meal without feeling as hungry as when he sat down. In the same way, though he loved fine horses and owned a stable full of thoroughbreds, he chose to ride the second best.

But, however abstemious, at least Thomas would have enjoyed the honour granted him at Lyons. As at the first Council there in 1245, he was made a papal chaplain. Pope Gregory, like Thomas with his horses, had an eye for outstanding quality.

The historian, T. F. Tout, suggests that Thomas went back to Oxford after the Council of Lyons to continue his role as Chancellor. On the other hand, Canon Capes, who wrote an account of Thomas's life as an introduction to his episcopal register, believes that after Lyons 'Cantilupe returned no more to any scene of Academic study, but gave more thought to the benefices which he held'. Whichever is true it could well be that Thomas made the most of summer weather to visit some of his more isolated livings, possibly those along the Welsh border. There he may have called on his sister, Juliana de Tregoz, who was married to the Lord of Ewyas, also, perhaps, on his old friend John le Breton, Bishop of Hereford. Through time, visiting his Marcher livings, he had come to know John le Breton well. They were both trained lawyers sharing an interest in church reform; at a guess they enjoyed each other's company. Certainly le Breton must have been impressed with Thomas for in 1273 he asked him, as a favour, to accept the appointment of Canon of Hereford Cathedral, as well as the prebend of Preston, a cathedral living.[4] He also asked him to be his successor. Thomas must have been touched by this last request, perhaps a little overwhelmed, but undoubtedly grateful. Possibly le Breton suspected he had not long to live and told Thomas so. Possibly also he explained that while the appointment to be prebend was not in doubt, there was a slight complication. The previous Bishop, Peter de Aquablanca, had already granted the prebend of Preston to a fellow countryman, Peter de Langon. It may have been because de Langon was French and chosen by Aquablanca that le Breton wanted to be rid of him. Soon afterwards de Langon appealed to Rome and the case went to the papal Curia. When Thomas was elected Bishop and, following the usual practice, gave up his livings and other appointments, he passed on the prebend of Preston to the Queen's chancellor, Henry de Woodstock. This apparently angered de Langon more than ever and caused Thomas much worry and unpleasantness not to mention exorbitant legal fees which continued to mount for the rest of his life. For owing to the snail-pace of the papal court, the case was not settled, till after his death – in de Langon's favour. De Langon was re-instated.

At last on 12th August 1274 Edward arrived in England. A week later he was crowned at Westminster. It was noticed with surprise, that Llywelyn, Prince of Wales, was not there. Llywelyn's absence was intentional, a deliberate gesture of independence from the man who, many years before, had been judged by Matthew Paris to be the most powerful Welsh leader since the Norman invasion. In return for his support in the civil war, Earl Simon had rewarded Llywelyn with the title, Prince of Wales. His betrothal to Simon's daughter, Eleanor, must have been intended to augment his power.

Remarkably, after the war Henry's government had allowed him to keep his title. There were, however, conditions. By the Treaty of Montgomery, the settlement worked out by Ottobuono in 1267, Llywelyn had to pay twenty thousand marks, in instalments, to the crown; he was also required to pay homage to any new King. Had he turned up for the new King's coronation, which would have been courteous and mannerly, he could have paid his homage to Edward. He could then have joined in the royal celebrations.

But Llywelyn had long distrusted Edward, suspecting him of deliberately detaining Eleanor de Montfort in England. He also resented the support given by the English to his outlawed brother, Dafydd. Edward should expect no homage from him till these grievances were dealt with satisfactorily.

Edward would not be dictated to. Nonetheless, the following summer, he accommodatingly came as far as Chester so that Llywelyn could perform his homage there. This was ignored, as were Edward's four subsequent summons. In November of the following year Edward would declare Llywelyn 'a rebel and disturber of the King's peace' and take steps to deal with him.

By that time the Welshman would also be proving a disturber of Thomas's peace.

John le Breton died at Hereford on 12th May 1275.

Though Thomas was his chosen successor there had to be an election. The day before it took place Thomas preached in the cathedral. According to Canon Capes there was no agreement at this first election but when a specially appointed committee of canons met on 15th June to make the decision, they elected Thomas overwhelmingly. But which Thomas? The cathedral records show that at that time there were at least two other canons belonging to the chapter named Thomas. According to one report when the result was announced, there were puzzled looks, murmurs of 'Which one? . . . Which Canon Thomas?'[5]

One of the others, Thomas de Saint Omer, later became an official of Archbishop Pecham and sided against Thomas in a dispute over a miracle cure at the Cathedral. Perhaps he felt bitter about the election for, when the votes were counted, the name of the next bishop was Canon Thomas Cantilupe.

Hearing the result Thomas is said to have been overcome with emotion; breaking down as he protested his unworthiness. He had been Chancellor of Oxford, Chancellor of all England, yet this appointment meant so much more to him. Perhaps he felt it came direct from God.

But Edward had no doubt of Thomas's worthiness. At once he accepted the Chapter's choice. Certainly Archbishop Kilwardby had no doubts about his former pupil's eligibility and, before long, news of acceptance arrived from Rome. A date was set for the consecration; it would take place on 8th September.

Perhaps the day was fine, cool and clear with a stiffish breeze that billowed the vestments of the many priests as they moved in slow procession towards the Cathedral. Behind them came the canons, archdeacons, bishops, the Archbishop himself, all resplendent in their ornamented copes. More than likely they entered through the great west doors so that as they approached they caught the glint of sunlight on the river Wye below them to the south. Above them the solid Norman tower stood out against the sky and had they looked beyond it they would have seen the tops of other towers, the crenellated drum towers of Hereford castle set on a rise above the Wye.

An impressive backdrop. The castle, one of the chain of border forts built by William FitzOsbern, the first Earl of Hereford, after the Conquest, was of major importance at that time of Welsh unrest. Thomas knew it well, had stayed there as part of the royal household, celebrating Mass in 'the fair and becoming chapel' which Henry had added in 1233. The cathedral too was familiar ground for he must often have paused there on his way to the livings he had held on the Welsh border for many years. Recently as a cathedral canon and prebend he would have taken part in the services. So it must already have meant a great deal to him, this towering sandstone building which had stood there for one hundred and forty years, though the see had been founded four centuries before. And that it was dedicated to the Virgin Mary, in tandem with Saint Ethelbert, made it special for Thomas; he was particularly devoted to the Blessed Mary.

Yet that day, as bishop, he would have seen it all from a new perspective; from that day this was his domain, his cathedral church, his diocese. It was an awesome responsibility. As bishop, he was not only landlord of vast estates, of twenty-three manors and hundreds of livings of various size, he was Pastor Pastorum, father-in-God to his numerous clergy, and, through them, to every parishioner. Besides these there were the various religious houses, the priories, monasteries and nunneries with every one of their occupants; he would now have charge over all of them.

The thought must have been in the forefront of his mind. And, as the procession entered the cathedral and made its way steadily up the nave, there they were on either side, faces turning to stare at him, his people packed into the pews, townsmen, country-men, parsons, friars, all of them curious, all, or most, willing to say their prayers for him.

And after the praying, the chanting of plainsong with incense drifting to the chancel roof, after the solemn oath of obedience, the promises, the blessing, would come the recessional down the nave, out through the doors, swung open now, out into the light and the clamour of bells. And there in the sunshine a waiting crowd, more of his people who had come to catch sight of their new Lord Bishop, a good man, they had heard, and an Englishman.

There would have been a celebration, a splendid banquet in honour of Archbishop Kilwardby, hosted by Thomas, who, presiding at a huge refectory table spread with vast quantities of food and wine, would eat and drink almost nothing himself. Among the visiting dignitaries were the Bishops of London and Rochester. Two bishops; only two. Where were all the rest?

The Archbishop was angry and he let it show. He was particularly indignant that neither the neigh-bouring Bishop of Worcester nor of Saint Asaph in Wales, nor the Abbot of Gloucester, had made the effort to come. A number of the bishops' registers for that year record letters of apology for their absence at Hereford on 8th September 1275.

For Thomas, however valid their excuses, for there to be so many absentees must have been a touch discouraging. A touch, no more. Thomas was spiritually robust enough not to allow himself to be distracted by his colleagues' offhandedness, or hostility even. He was experienced at handling problems of all kinds, political, human, theological. He must have expected to face many more in the time ahead. A look through his bishop's register makes it clear he did.

Chapter VII

bishop's register was a record of the administration of the diocese; the entries include letters, appointments, writs, all of which deal with an enormous range of issues from ordinations to the fabric of a church. It sounds dull, dry, pages of facts, which indeed it is, but it does give an insight into the power of the medieval church, its influence, wealth, how it organized its clergy and coped with corruption. From it also can be culled an idea of the life Bishop Thomas led, his frequent journeying from place to place, the various problems he came up against.

The keeping of a register was a relatively new practice in Thomas's day. He is thought to have introduced the idea to Hereford for his is the earliest to have survived. The register is not a massive tome and is by no means a complete record of Thomas's episcopate. A great many documents are known to have been stored in boxes or chests and kept in the cathedral chapter house together with the records of previous bishops, a great accumulation of material, most of which has disappeared. When they accompanied

Thomas on his travels the clerks took a minimum of documents. The register, containing the currently important items, was a convenient way of managing this, the contemporary way, the medieval compact disc. As it stands the register consists of about seventy parchment folios between leather-covered boards which measure roughly twelve inches by seven. It must have been written by a number of clerks for the handwriting varies – one entry is thought to be in Thomas's own hand. The contents are mainly chronological though in places there are muddles, the order is wrong, entries are crossed out, spaces left blank; there are also insertions, whole pages added and stitched in place. Matters of particular importance, or rather, those the scribes judged to be so, are indicated by a small drawing of a pointed finger. For the first three years entries are divided under separate headings; legal matters, estate administration, visitations. Then this orderly method falls apart, entries are mixed. Perhaps the clerks had no time to sort them out, perhaps they were short-staffed, lazy, slow. We shall never know. But the imperfections somehow make it more human; they bring it to life.

One of the earliest entries, dated 10th August 1275, acknowledges the receipt from the Chapter of two mitres, a pastoral staff and a ring left by preceding bishops for their successors to use in office. All are to be returned at his death unless the Abbot of Reading shall have claimed the staff.

A great many entries are financial and it is clear that, as a bishop, Thomas was less well off than he had been before. He no longer had the income from the many livings he had now relinquished and, though he owned considerable inherited wealth, it was mainly in land. Hereford was not a rich diocese;

his successor, Richard Swinfield, complained that it was the worst endowed bishopric in England. In fact that distinction went to Rochester, which according to the tax records, the *Taxatio Nicholai*, for 1291 had an income of £183 10s 7d. In the same year the income for Winchester, the richest see, was roughly £3,000. Hereford is put at £449 1s 5d.

A bishop's income came principally from the manors and estates belonging to the see. Hereford owned twenty-three manors and a great extent of land but because much of it lay along the Welsh border with the constant threat of plunder from rebellious Welshmen, the taxable value was rated low. On the debit side the manors with their adjoining farms incurred enormous costs; there were wages, building repairs, the restocking of farms. Thomas found he was obliged to pay off a number of debts left by his predecessor, John le Breton; one, a large outlay of stock, he did not manage to settle until 1278. In fact, having used up his savings, Thomas was forced to borrow money. His register shows that in 1276 William de Rotherfield, Dean of York, lent him a hundred pounds (Thomas had been a canon of York). In 1279 there were several loans, one from the executors of his brother, Hugh, for £102 6s 6d, one of one hundred marks from Canon Peter of Chester, another of eighty marks from John de Clare, and, with the consent of the Hereford Chapter, two hundred marks from a reserve deposit in the treasury.

The heaviest outlay for any bishop was his staff; not only their wages but their total upkeep, their clothing, food and drink. And there were dozens of them, hundreds even.

All bishops required a legal staff and, though, except for his final journal, almost nothing has survived of Thomas's household accounts, with his numerous cases grinding through the courts, he would have needed at least five advocates in his service in the King's Bench alone. Besides these there were proctors, attorneys, sequestrators and penitentiaries (who dealt with questions of penance). And, of course, each legal officer had to have a clerk. Thomas also employed his own champion, a stalwart named Thomas de Bruges, who would settle a dispute by fighting a duel. Most important were the ecclesiastical staff, who would deal with the administration of the diocese while Thomas was travelling, which his register shows was most of the time. Among those he appointed were friends and associates of high calibre, university graduates such as his kinsman, William de Montfort (the son of Peter de Montfort of Beaudesert), Robert of Gloucester, also known as Robert le Wyse (who Canon Capes believes was probably the same person as the chronicler of that name) and Luke de Bré. Besides these officials there were chaplains, the clerks of the chapel, also several friars. We know that Thomas, who, as an aristocrat, spoke Norman French, always travelled with a Franciscan friar who would translate his preaching into English, the everyday language of the commoners. Most often this was his confessor, the Franciscan, Henry de Bellington, who, according to a witness at the canonization hearings, was 'an excellent preacher in the English tongue.'[1]

Yet another group of employees were the men who looked after the estates,[2] an enormous number whose work ranged from accounting and auditing, to foresters and fowlers. Between were the keepers, stewards and bailiffs; these were duplicated on each estate.

Those closest to the master, those Thomas would have known best, were his household, the *familia*, which consisted of about forty men strictly graded as to seniority. Chief among them were his personal clerics, his chaplain and the clerks, who served his spiritual needs. Then came the squires, each earning about fifteen shillings a year, then the valets, employees such as the clerk of the chapel, huntsmen, farriers and larderers, who would earn between five and eight shillings. Next came the servants; the kitchen and cleaning staff, outdoor workers and undergrooms. Last were the pages, young boys taken on as apprentices.

When Thomas travelled round his diocese his household went with him, loading the baggage onto horse-drawn wagons and trundling off to another of his manors, or palaces, as bishops' residences were known. The resident staff would have everything prepared, there would be food, fuel and, *Deo volente*, unblocked drains. One of the finest of the episcopal residences was Bosbury, said to have been 'a fayre palace' at the time of King Offa five centuries before, but still fair enough in Thomas's day and conveniently close to Ledbury where the vineyards produced a palatable white wine. According to the register, on 24th November 1276, Thomas was authorized by papal bull to use the income from the churches at Ledbury and Bosbury for the costs of the episcopal *mensa*, literally his table, in reality his household expenses. He simply could not manage otherwise to provide for his great army of employees and to entertain, on the previous allowance. And Thomas almost always did entertain wherever he went, and did so generously, unlike some bishops who, on a visitation, would expect to be wined and dined in style, a daunting prospect for most parish priests, whose incomes were wretchedly inadequate.

Another palace was at Whitbourne on the Worcestershire border, where the neighbouring Brinkestye wood was a ready source of game and the moat was stocked with fish, though Thomas never seemed to stop there long. Two other manors where he often stayed were at Bishop's Castle in the north of the diocese, and Stretton Sugwas, which was only four miles from Hereford. Here the manor, set deep in its great wooded park, felt secluded and peaceful. Thomas needed that, the serenity, the chance to be alone however brief. He grew fond of Stretton Sugwas and, long after he died, in the fifteenth century, a stained glass window in his memory was put into the chapel. Later the glass was moved to the east window of the parish church at Ross-on-Wye.

Thomas seldom stayed at his Hereford palace. It was not that the city did not concern him. In fact he worked hard to establish diocesan rights against various infringements; matters such as the customs and rights of traders and townsfolk at the street fairs. But he preferred to do so from Stretton Sugwas, to keep the cathedral at arms length. The cathedral, after all, came under the administration of the dean, as it does today.

The dean at the time happened to be John de Aquablanca, nephew of Peter de Aquablanca. Thomas knew all too well about Bishop de Aquablanca, the Savoyard who had preceded John le Breton and who had appointed his fellow country-man, Peter de Langon, to be prebend of Preston. Thomas had been his duplicate. It was a problem currently causing Thomas considerable anguish and one of his most intractable. That was not the only problem Thomas had inherited from Bishop de Aquablanca, who had been notorious for procuring rewarding positions for his many relations. This had made him deeply unpopular, the most unpopular prelate in England, it was said. Matthew Paris denigrates the Savoyard for speaking no English,[3] though, in fact, the language of the Church was Latin and that of the nobility was Norman French. He also notes that the bishop exhaled 'a foul and sulphurous stench'. Perhaps this was caused by the enormous growth inside his nose and the fact that he was grossly overweight. He seems to have spent most of his time abroad, making money it was said, and living extremely well. Meanwhile his relations ran the diocese. Regrettably for Thomas, when he became bishop, a number of them were still there.

Besides the dean there was Emery, Chancellor of Hereford, another nephew of Bishop Peter's; there were three great-nephews, James de Aquablanca, Archdeacon of Shropshire, Peter and Pontius de Salins, who held livings and numerous portions (parts of divided livings). There were also many friends and associates of the bishop, including his physician, Master Caturmus, the Rector of Eastnor, who, the register reveals, was given five years leave to go on crusade provided he found a dependable replacement and gave half a mark of silver to the poor of the parish for each year he was away. Others were Gerard de Eugines, Rector of Colwall, Vicini de Conflens, Martin de Chambery, Hugh de Tournon . . . the list goes on and on.

Thomas was not opposed to foreigners, nor to foreign clergy in his diocese, provided they cared for their parishioners. It was those who failed to do so that Thomas refused to tolerate. They were by no

means all Aquablanca relations. There were numerous priests who neglected their livings, others who
procured them without proper dispensation, there
were those guilty of simony (the buying and selling
of privileges or pardons), and that included friars; all
of them deserved to be thrown out. Thomas set about
doing so with typical vigour; he was thorough and
persistent, ruthless, you could say. It was hardly
surprising that his victims, and others, accused him
of being a hypocrite. Who was he to talk of being a
pluralist? Such criticism did not deter Thomas.
Suspected transgressors – his officials were encouraged to act as sleuths – would be investigated and
those found guilty disciplined accordingly. As the
clergy were exempt from secular courts this was
normally done through the bishop's court which had
extensive powers.[4] Clergy might be suspended from
their livings, or deprived altogether; sometimes their
goods would be confiscated; hardened offenders
could be sent to the bishop's prison.[5] Errant friars and
monks would either end up there or find themselves
expelled from the diocese.

When it came to dealing with the Aquablanca clan
Thomas came up against difficulties. James, the great-
nephew of Bishop Peter, who had been Archdeacon
of Shropshire since he was a schoolboy, was cited by
Thomas to answer charges of pluralism and non-resi-
dence. (He was away being educated for five years.)
Though Thomas dislodged James eventually, the case
dragged on for a very long time.

Thomas lost out over Peter and Pontius. Their
uncle Emery, the Chancellor of Hereford, intervened.
Peter and Pontius kept their livings, every one of
them.

The position of John de Aquablanca was more

complicated. When Thomas became bishop the office of dean was being challenged by Giles de Avenbury who, having held it earlier, had been forced to resign and had then been reinstated, or so he claimed. In the meantime John had been appointed as dean by his uncle, the bishop. The case had been referred to the papal court. Thomas, concerned at the uncertainty, intervened. He tried to arrange a temporary solution, without success. The feuding generated bitterness. Soon many in the Chapter were involved. It developed into a serious distraction from the clerics' duties in the church. That was what Thomas cared about.

The Roman Curia judged in favour of John de Aquablanca – in 1282, the year Thomas died. So he had no relief from the feuding deans. Perhaps he saw the fraughtness as a kind of penance, a cerebral hairshirt to be endured for the glory of God.

Despite the pressures of the diocese Thomas, as a member of the King's council, was duty bound to attend parliaments and councils all over the country. More often than not parliaments were held at Westminster which meant making the long journey from the Marches to London. Thomas would often stop en route at Earley, near Reading, where he leased a house, which it seems he later bought as he left it to his sister, Juliana de Tregoz. A number of letters in the register were written from Earley, also from Tottenhalle, now Tottenham, less than seven miles from Westminster. Thomas is thought to have had lodgings there, or possibly a house, leased from the prior and canons of Holy Trinity within Aldgate. More likely when in London he would stay at the episcopal residence, Montalt, on Old Fish Street Hill, where he would entertain in style, as he always did. He seems to have been happy to be in London;

perhaps he felt so more than ever now, welcoming the break from his diocese, the sense of being back at the heart of things, of meeting his friends; the statesmen, the magnates, the greatest in the land, of which he was undoubtedly one. And, humble though he was, in the words of Richard Strange, 'was not puffed up, like many, with fumes of swelling exaltation ...', he must have been well aware of his status, even, discreetly, relished it. Certainly Edward valued him as a councillor. Being the bishop of a border diocese, his advice was particularly important at that time when Prince Llywelyn of Wales was increasingly militant. Thomas was present at the council in November 1276, when Llywelyn was condemned as a rebel, adding his signature to the official letter, warning the Welshman he had gone too far.

The following July Edward launched his first attack on Llywelyn, driving him into north west Wales. By the Treaty of Aberconwy Llywelyn was forced to agree that this region alone constituted his much reduced principality. At last, having sworn fealty to Edward, peace was made and the following year his marriage to Eleanor de Montfort went ahead. The wedding was at Worcester – Thomas was almost certainly there – a fine ceremony, paid for by Edward, a demonstration of his friendship for Llywelyn. The goodwill was superficial, it did not last and a few months later rebellion broke out again.

The situation did not improve until, following Edward's Welsh campaign, the principality was united under the crown. The Statute of Wales was signed in 1284, two years after Thomas died. Which meant that the danger of attack along the western border of his diocese lasted throughout his episcopacy.

On another historic occasion in September 1278, Thomas watched Alexander, the King of the Scots, pay homage to Edward at the Westminster parliament. In April 1279 Edward underlined his admiration for Thomas by appointing him as one of his regents, a royal *locum tenens*, while he was away in France. Thomas's father had held the same position in 1242.

A quality Edward must have particularly valued in Thomas was his independent mind; he stood by what he believed to be right. On one occasion when they disagreed, Edward conceded to Thomas's view, very much as when Thomas, as Chancellor, had refused to seal a letter for Edward's father. This time the sticking point for Thomas was Edward's intention to allow a Jew to act as a witness against Christians. The Jew was a convert, the Christians were forgers, yet, Judge Ralph of Hengham,[6] who was there at the time, told how Thomas wept as he begged Edward to release him from the council rather than give a Jew power over a Christian.[7] Afterwards, with Edward's permission, he preached to them, sternly rejecting the gifts they offered him.

Thomas's anti-Semitism was not exceptional. In the twelfth century Jewish financiers had been extremely successful particularly in their dealings with the Church, mainly in loans enabling the purchase of land. This had given them considerable power which, combined with their being an alien race, had led to their intense unpopularity and, in the thirteenth century, to their exploitation and persecution. In 1256 the normally good relations between the citizens of London and the Franciscan and Dominican friars had been at risk of breaking down when the friars, bravely, attempted to treat the Jews as human beings.

In the eyes of the Church Jews, the whole race, were the murderers of Christ – a case of the sins of the fathers.

There was one member of Edward's council who, it must be true to say, counted Thomas as his arch-enemy. The Earl of Gloucester, Gilbert de Clare knew that Thomas did not trust him for several reasons, principally for his betrayal of Earl Simon; his switching of allegiance to the royalists had tilted the balance at Evesham. Perhaps when they met at councils and parliaments, the arrogant young Earl would disdain to speak to Thomas, or to meet his eye, an indication of his hatred – and his guilt.

For many years the Earls of Gloucester had claimed the right to hunt over the Eastnor and Colwall chase above Ledbury. The present Earl had always hunted there. This was, in fact, church land; it belonged to the Hereford diocese but no previous bishop had challenged the trespass. Thomas did. When it came to defending the rights of the Church he was prepared to challenge anyone. In October 1275, probably as soon as Thomas learned of the trespass, he summoned the Earl, who failed to appear. Thomas summoned him again; he did so repeatedly. Each time the Earl postponed his appearance. Perhaps he enjoyed baiting the bishop he so despised. Thomas did not hesitate to take out legal proceedings against him. It was after the King had ordered him to remove his foresters that, finally, on a cold January day in 1278, Thomas met a number of justices with a jury on the chase to settle the matter. Having heard of this the Earl appeared, with a full force of retainers, brandishing a writ which he claimed was from Edward allowing yet another postponement. While the judges made their inspection, Thomas with his clergy retired to a nearby wood, put on his full regalia, and, with mitre and crozier, returned to the judges and the Earl. Hugh le Barber who was there, told the canonization commissioners how, when the justices gave their verdict in favour of Thomas,[8] the Earl became abusive, threatening Thomas with *multa verba imperiosa et superba*, calling him a 'clergiaster' and vowing to castigate him and all his kind. Thomas stood up to this onslaught with dignified calm. 'My lord,' he replied in Richard Strange's version of the story, 'say what you please of me, you shall never provoke me to say anything against you misbeseeming; that's not the thing I come for, but to recover the rights of my Church.' Then, having pronounced excommunication on the Earl and his retainers, he called on his waiting huntsmen and hounds and for three consecutive days he hunted over the entire chase to prove his point. It is said that the deep trench in the Malvern hills was dug by the Earl's men to mark the division of diocesan land from his own.

There are two sequels to the story; one tells of how a number of the Earl of Gloucester's retainers, rough foresters, insolent and hostile, had been so overawed by Thomas's sentence of excommunication, that, long afterwards, they came to beg for absolution. The other comes from Richard Strange, who maintains that when, after Thomas died, Gilbert de Clare came to Hereford Cathedral and looked at Thomas's bones, they began to bleed. He was 'much amazed hereat . . . was struck with compunction . . .'.

The register gives evidence of another dispute involving Gilbert de Clare, which had been simmering alongside the Malvern Down affair. In July 1277 Edward held a council, an assembly of magnates, as the register puts it, at Worcester and arrangements were made a whole year before for Thomas to lodge nearby at the hospice at Powick. Thomas then learned that the lodgings had been assigned to Gilbert de Clare, who had every intention of using them. If Thomas uttered curses, and, according to Hugh le Barber, the only oath he was ever heard to use was 'by Saint Dewy', he must have uttered it with feeling then. He also sent off a petition to Edward who promptly re-assigned the lodgings to him. The Earl of Gloucester's curses, when he heard of this, must have been a good deal stronger than 'by Saint Dewy'.

Thomas would have seen it as a victory for the Church, with perhaps a very small sense of self-satisfaction; he was human after all.

At the same time in the north of the diocese Thomas was confronting another of the powerful Marcher lords over disputed boundaries. Peter Corbet, Baron of Caus, owned extensive lands around Lydbury along the Welsh border of Shropshire. The Corbets, high-born Normans, had arrived with the Conqueror and built a great stronghold commanding the valley of the Rea. For decades they had put up with aggression from the Welsh, losing cattle and land. But on their eastern boundary, perhaps to compensate, they had themselves encroached and on a massive scale. Four hundred acres of pasturage belonging to the Church had been annexed by the Corbet family. The register contains a writ issued on 8th May 1276, summoning Peter Corbet to appear before the Justices of Westminster. Over two years later, after further writs complaining of his failure to appear at Westminster, as well as failure to attend the perambulation of the boundaries of the disputed territory 'withon the Sheriff of Shropshire and a jury of belted knights', the King's court pronounced their finding. They found for Thomas. The four hundred acres were returned to the Church; the boundaries were fixed.

They were not fixed as far as Llywelyn was concerned. He had helped himself to extensive lands along the border close to Montgomery. It was an area that had changed sides several times, most recently during the civil war when it was taken by Llywelyn and then granted to him under the Treaty of Montgomery – or so he claimed. A bogus claim, Thomas declared; the land with its three 'vills' (manors with their adjoining farms) Chastroke, Aston and Muliton, belonged to the Church. The Register shows that as early as September 1275, he launched a campaign to have them restored. At his instigation, his good friend, Archbishop Kilwardby, wrote to Llywelyn urging him to return the lands. Llywelyn took no notice. Thomas persisted, with letter after letter, with legislation, finally, with excommunication of the tenants of the vills, who were resisting what the register terms 'episcopal control'. At one point Thomas occupied the castle at Lydbury and was surrounded by an army of Welshmen. Thomas's servant, Hugh le Barber, who was there at the time, gave a rather confused account of what happened at the canonization hearings. He remembered how candles had been planted in a ditch close to the castle, many hundreds of candles which, after dark, appeared like the lights of a formidable army lying in wait. The Welshmen, terrified, fled into the hills while the inhabitants of the vills, daring to emerge, signalled that they wanted to make peace. Whether Thomas then absolved them from excommunication Hugh did not say, but he added that they were given protection, with their families and cattle, within the castle, and when the lord Thomas recovered the rights to the land, which eventually he did, he held the vills in peace.

Perhaps even bishops were bound to find it difficult to love each other when the boundaries of their neighbouring dioceses were not clearly defined. This was true of many boundaries in the early Middle Ages and was certainly the case with the western side of the Hereford diocese when Thomas took over the episcopacy. Almost at once he became involved in a dispute with Anian Sais, the fiery Bishop of Saint Asaph. Anian, who had returned from crusade to confrontation with Llywelyn, was renowned for rushing headlong into litigation. He did so with Thomas over several parishes in a part of Montgomery known as Gordwr, which Thomas claimed belonged to Hereford. The case was referred to the papal court and the register records letter after letter from Thomas to his proctors in Rome. Towards the end of his episcopacy, Thomas wrote instructing them to arrange gifts for the cardinals dealing with his case. He informs them that, at the time, he can afford only one hundred pounds, which should be given to the most influential cardinals. And, while he dislikes giving money or jewels to the Pope, if absolutely necessary the amount required must be borrowed.

Which, knowing Thomas, seems hardly credible. But the cardinals in Rome were far from impartial, backhanders happened, were routine even, and Thomas was convinced that he was in the right; it was for the sake of the Church, the bribery. God would understand.

Eventually the Pope passed the case to the Archbishop of Canterbury, who by then was John Pecham, no friend of Thomas. A Court of Arbitration was set up but it was not until 1288 that agreement was finally reached. On 25th November, at Bishop's Castle, Richard Swinfield, Thomas's successor, took possession of 'all parishes to the east of the River Severn from a point near Montgomery to Shrawardine ...'

In the south-west of the diocese Thomas tangled with another bishop. This time it was Thomas Bek, Bishop of Saint David's, who contested Thomas's claim to the Abbey of Dore. At an unknown date – there is no mention of it in the register – Thomas was asked to consecrate this beautiful building, the recently completed church of the monastery founded in the mid-twelfth century. Bishop Bek protested. Perhaps he warned Thomas to keep away. It seems likely, however, that Thomas already expected trouble for, when it came, an armed attack as he travelled to Dore, it was led by his nephew, Baron de Tregoz.

Thomas must have known of his nephew's alliance with Bishop Bek. He must also have been distressed by it, for he was close to his sister, Juliana de Tregoz – or had been until recently. It could be that his refusal to embrace her since becoming a bishop, his apparent sudden coldness towards her, had, through the years, gradually changed her feelings towards him, causing her to turn away from him. Had she known in advance of her son's proposed attack and closed her eyes to it? If her pious brother was so close to God, God would surely take care of him.

Apparently He did. Somehow Thomas reached Dore and carried out the consecration, re-enforcing his episcopal right to Dore.

In fact it was not until long after Thomas's death that jurisdiction over Dore was finally made – in favour of Hereford.[9]

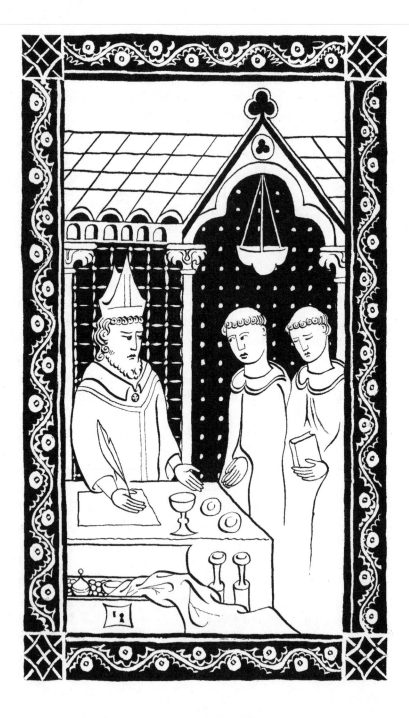

CHAPTER VIII

I n the thirteenth century the Hereford diocese covered an enormous area. It spread beyond the borders of Hereford-shire to include parishes in south-west Shrop-shire, in Worcestershire and Gloucestershire, as well as those across the Welsh border claimed by Thomas as part of his see. In 1291 there were about three hundred and forty parishes. Many were poor and isolated, a cluster of small dwellings, a primitive church. For the priest-in-charge, cut off from the outside world, it was a lonely life. Thomas was very much aware of this and did all he could to provide support and encouragement.

An opportunity to do so should have occurred at the diocesan synod or council – the word synod comes from the Greek *synodos*, meeting – which met annually, usually in the autumn.[1] In theory all the clergy in the diocese would attend; in reality only a small proportion did. The prospect of travelling often many miles through wild countryside and then paying for lodgings in order to sit through several days of wordy debate on church legislation was enough to put off all but the most assiduous priests. Those with grievances, those most in need of spiritual and practical help, were probably the poorest and so least likely to come. It was therefore up to Thomas to visit his clergy in their parishes and, as his register shows, he spent the seven years of his episcopacy travelling from place to place, seldom staying anywhere for more than a few days. In 1276, his first full year in office, he moved thirty-four times, the following year the number was the same, in 1278 it was thirty-seven. And, while some of his journeys were to parliaments and councils, wherever Edward held them, the majority were round his diocese.

Giving evidence at the canonization hearing Hugh le Barber told the judges that Thomas was 'diligent in visitation'. But Hugh's memory was hazy, there was nothing more specific; it was all too long ago. Unfortunately Thomas's visitation rolls, the record of his parish visiting, have disappeared, but those of other bishops have survived, including that of his successor, Richard Swinfield.[2] The usual pattern was for a bishop to visit each parish in his diocese every three years. Of course this did not always happen; some bishops were otherwise occupied. In 1240 Ralph de Neville, Bishop of Chichester, was also Chancellor of England, while some, like Bishop Giffard of Worcester, were elderly and in poor health.

Each visitation was planned in advance. This was necessary, for the bishop was not simply calling on the priest, he was carrying out an official inspection. And it was not only the priest who was involved, his deacon, sub-deacon, chaplains and churchwardens, as well as the church building and all that went with it, came under careful scrutiny.

Generally, a few weeks before his visit, the bishop would send the rural dean or archdeacon to the parish armed with a check list of relevant questions.[3] What was the financial state of the church? Was the inventory up to date? Was there an inventory at all? What was the condition of the buildings? Was there evidence of witchcraft, concubinage, illegitimacy, misuse of the churchyard? The enquiry was wide ranging and detailed and it must have been tempting to fudge the answers, to conceal and deceive. There was really no point. The bishop, certainly one as rigorous as Thomas, would use the dean's report merely as a briefing, a foretaste of what to expect. The discerning bishop would judge for himself.

He would arrive as arranged, or thereabouts – travelling time was unpredictable – with his retinue, some of whom would most likely have been sent on in advance to prepare accommodation and stock up with provisions. The bishop would often entertain his host, at his own expense, at other times he and his officers would be provided with bed and board, a crippling expense for the poorly paid priest.

The Household Roll of Thomas's successor, Richard Swinfield, provides details of a visitation tour of the diocese made in 1290, illustrating how in some parishes, Bromyard, for example, he and his whole retinue were entertained by one of the priests who held the living. At Kinlet, near Bewdley, he spent two nights at his own expense, though as he was presented with capons, kids and venison, as well as flour and fuel, that cannot have been a problem. All the same the fact that Robert the carter had to travel on to Kidderminster to buy the rest of the food, paying a guide one penny to lead him through Wyre forest, illustrates the isolation of such villages, and the difficulty of finding the way through unknown and densely wooded countryside.

It would probably be the morning after his arrival that the bishop would begin his inspection. With his officers in tow, he would tour the churchyard, check the gravestones, the lych-gate, the outer wall; then investigate the church, everything about it from the lead on the roof to the freshness of the eucharistic wine. He would count the Mass books, the purificators and the chalices, look closely at the vestments and surplices. When it came to the priest, by this time probably sweating quite a bit, there would be questioning. If the bishop was Thomas, this would be done kindly, but searchingly and in such a way, earnestly with steady eye contact, that deception would be impossible.

Thomas – any bishop – would meet the parishioners, visit the sick and present them with gifts. He might consecrate a church or a chantry chapel, he would celebrate the Mass. This he always did with such heartfelt emotion, 'ecstatic fervour' as T. F. Tout describes it, that tears would run down his cheeks. With equal fervour he would preach (in Latin or French with a translation by Henry de Bellington), he would also hear confessions, baptize and confirm.

In the thirteenth century children were confirmed when they were very young, often as babies, too young for any kind of preparation. Confirmation seems to have been regarded as an extension of baptism, an endorsement by the bishop of the earlier rite performed by the parish priest. Thomas always wore his stole when he rode round his diocese so that should he meet anyone who wanted him to confirm their child, he was able to do so there and then.[4]

With such on the spot alfresco confirmations – 'a somewhat rough and ready system' in the words of Canon Capes – it is hardly surprising there is no record of them in the register. Ordinations, however, are certainly included, pages of carefully written lists, some of which are missing, giving the date, place, the names of those ordained followed by their titles, (income or means of support) divided into separate categories; sub-deacons, deacons, priests and, sometimes, acolytes (assistants).[5] For example at Leominster, on 18th September 1277, Thomas ordained thirty-five subdeacons, thirty-six deacons and twenty-seven priests; a year later, at Ludlow, he worked overtime ordaining fifty-two acolytes, thirty-five sub-deacons and twenty-seven priests, ten of them without titles. This could prove expensive for, in theory, the bishop was personally responsible for supporting those he ordained without an adequate income, until they found employment. Thomas, with his strange mix of saintly compassion and financial astuteness, took great care to protect himself against any long term commitment. For instance a deacon, Simon Franc, who, according to the register, was ordained *sine titulo* by Thomas at Tottenham on 13th June 1278, was obliged to swear an oath that he would not claim support from Thomas in the future. If this seems callous on Thomas's part, he was, in fact, by then being forced to borrow to pay his enormous legal costs. Besides as, in this case, Thomas was standing in for the Bishop of London and the deacon, Simon Franc, belonged to the Lincoln diocese, an opt-out doesn't seem unreasonable.

Overall, however, Thomas's first concern was for the Church, for the well-being of the religious life of his diocese. Which meant, wherever possible, getting rid of those found to be corrupt and replacing them with men of good character, and ensuring each one was properly ordained. His register contains a letter to his official insisting on the importance of ordination 'of whatever rank the man might be'.

Thomas took great care to match a new incumbent to a living. A poor and isolated parish needed a priest who was practical and physically strong; a graduate would be a pointless waste. There were, after all, few enough of them. Records show that of the ninety-nine men ordained by Thomas at Leominster in 1277, two had degrees, only two. Of the other two hundred and seventy-five ordained by Thomas within the Hereford diocese, not one was a graduate.

Ordinations were held four times a year on Ember Days[6] and took place wherever Thomas happened to be on his travels. That no ordinations were at Hereford is perhaps no surprise; he spent as little time there as possible. Some weeks before the date of the ordination, notice would be circulated round the diocese summoning candidates to present themselves for examination. It seems Thomas recruited his episcopal officers to carry this out, for an entry in the register directs one of these officers 'to pay no regard to rank in citations for Holy Orders'. Selection should depend on fitness for office; status should have no part in it, nor should influence and wealth, whatever the potential benefits. They did, of course; though probably less under Thomas, than under many other bishops.

Thomas would also have taken part in assessing prospective ordinands, probably interviewing those shortlisted by his officers. And while their class did not concern him, their background did; were they, for instance, illegitimate? If so, official dispensation from

Rome was required. Nonetheless, and often without consent from Rome, noblemen would try to park their bastards on the Church. The register includes a letter written in April 1277, from Pope John XXI asking Thomas to judge the suitability of Peter de Llanrothal, who was illegitimate, for Holy Orders. Having done so Thomas instructed Peter to study singing for a year, after which, no longer musically challenged, Peter was ordained. Another drawback was physical imperfection, though for a minor defect the Pope would grant dispensation. This was allowed for a certain John of Ditenshale, who had one finger cut short by an unskilled surgeon. There was also Robert who, despite a defect on the pupil of one eye, was allowed to become the Rector of Fownhope.

The ordination lists in Thomas's register show that the majority of priests have *ad titulum patriomonii* after their names. They were parochial priests, parsons of country parishes, whose appointment did not depend only on Thomas or his officials. The patron, almost always the local lord, had the right to appoint the parish priest though the bishop might not always approve of his choice. As the register reveals Thomas was charged by Theobald de Verdun with interfering in his rights as patron. Having appeared before the royal justices at Shrewsbury to answer the charge, Thomas lost the case. In another disagreement with a patron in May 1278, Thomas set up an enquiry into the advowson (the right to recommend a priest to a living) of Much Marcle. Sometimes a dispute would be settled with a proviso or condition. For example, Henry of Upavene could be appointed to Hopesay provided he learned plainsong. Sometimes the ordinand was too young, in which case a decision about his future would be delayed until he had completed his education. An instance of this was Hugh Burnell, the nominee to the church of Chetton, who according to the register, was 'under age and absent'.

The lists also show very few livings provided by monasteries or priories; there are ten in Thomas's ordination lists. One reason for this was that in the 13th century, despite their apparent prosperity, religious houses had suffered from bouts of crippling taxation. In his chronicle Matthew Paris points out the injustice of this financial burden.

When Thomas first took office he found the Benedictine priory of Leominster in such financial trouble that on 26th December it was taken under royal protection. Perhaps Thomas, as one of Edward's councillors had suggested the idea. The register notes that Sir Roland de Harley was given custody of the estates belonging to the priory and was 'to provide for necessary wants and the poor'. In 1279 the situation at the Monmouth priory was equally desperate and, though not recorded in the register, it is known that Thomas issued an indulgence in its favour, relieving them of debt.

In the autumn of 1277 Thomas visited two Augustinian priories, one at Chirbury in south Shropshire the other at Wormsley to the west of Hereford. He found both in such serious financial trouble that they were directed to admit no more canons without his consent. Debt, however, was not the only problem. At Wormsley Thomas insisted that rules of silence must be better observed and that 'no women should stay at night within the walls'. Worse still at Chirbury where he learned of such 'notorious scandals' that the Prior was ordered to have the buildings securely enclosed and to check 'the access of women'. He adds that if they must speak to laymen on business matters they should do so in the parish church or the graveyard. Furthermore a report was to be made of punishments meted out to transgressors.

The misdemeanours of the sisters of the small Augustinian priory at Limebrook must have seemed mild in comparison. Indeed after his visitation to their remote house near Lingen, he wrote a long letter to them expressing his pleasure at 'the zeal and loving union of which I found evidence'. At the same time he reminds them of their rules of silence and the Rule of their order. These sisters, believed to be of noble birth, were anchoresses, solitaries who devoted their days to contemplation and prayer. But, as most of them were young and possibly comely, did Thomas suspect that visitors and servants, even their Confessors, stayed rather longer than they needed to, that the sisters did not always limit themselves strictly to 'the fitting uses of the chapter house, the cloister, refectory and dormitory?' Furthermore could it be that gifts were accepted, even adornments and 'presents for dress?' Judging from the exhortations in his letter to avoid these sins, the answer is yes. But he urges gently, with encouragement, thoughtfully requesting that his letter be read aloud in both English and French to ensure that all should understand. One has the feeling he enjoyed his visit, the sisters had given him 'joy in Christ'. It seems they also gave him a copy of *Ancrene Wisse*, their handbook or guide – 'wisse' is an Anglo Saxon word – for a direct quote from the book, that the sisters should 'guard the gates of their senses' appears in his letter. The *Ancrene Wisse* is one of six manuscripts discovered some thirty years ago in various libraries, which, after intensive sleuthing by Professor E. J. Dobson, who honed his code-breaking skills in the secret service during the war, were found to be by a secular canon from Wigmore Abbey, Brian of Lingen, confessor to the sisters at Limebrook. Unusually all six are written in English rather than Latin in prose so vivid and readable it must surely have appealed to the young anchoresses.[7]

It would be heartening to think that, as he rode away, he allowed himself to dream of these lively girls exchanging their rosaries for pretty beads and laughing and singing as they danced through the cloister and chapter house. Heartening, maybe, but improbable. Women were weak and wayward creatures, even these sisters were daughters of Eve.

This point of view must have been confirmed by a scandal that came to light in the last year of his episcopacy, the kind of incident which now would be headline news. An entry in the register dated 13th January 1282, notes that William de Wynton, subprior of Leominster, was cited to appear before the Bishop to answer for 'alleged incontinence with a nun of Lingebroke (Limebrook), and other women'. Having failed to appear William had been excommunicated and fined. But he appealed to Rome, confident, perhaps, that his case would be buried in the papal Curia for many years. The register does not mention the nun. Was she given comfort or punished for her sin? Was there a birth at Lingebroke?

The problems at Wormsley, Chirbury and Limebook were all concerned with internal discipline. At Leominster there were problems of a different kind; the most intractable involved the Benedictine monks, the people of the town and the priory church. It was a longstanding problem that had existed since the church was completed in the middle of the twelfth century. Built by Henry I, who also founded the monastery, the neighbouring church was in the same

Romanesque style as his great abbey at Reading. Both churches were on a magnificent scale, indeed, apart from the Cathedral, the Leominster church was the largest in Herefordshire. So that, as the townspeople had no parish church, it must have seemed an obvious solution for them to share it with the monks. However when they were granted the right to hold services in the western end of the nave, the monks objected. Despite the fact that they had the whole of the rest of this large church, there was protest, argument, ill feeling on both sides. After a time another nave was added, replacing the south aisle, for the use of the parish. The hostility went on.

It was probably January 1276 – there seems to be some confusion about the date – when Thomas came to Leominster to sort the matter out. It was a formal visitation. Arriving with his full retinue he was received by the prior and conducted to the church where he preached to the assembled monks. He then took the prior and subprior aside for interrogation, while his officers and clerks questioned the monks. The enquiry concerned the parishioners' access to the church. Why were the main doors kept locked? Why were the bells not rung at service times? The parishioners had provided the bells, paid for them out of their earnings. No wonder they were angry. Thomas made his disapproval clear. He forbade the locking of the church doors and ordered the proper use of the bells. He also pointed out that almsgiving had declined, that endowments had been 'misapplied' – it is not hard to imagine how – and that both these matters must be put right at once.

Thomas followed up his visit with a long letter setting out his instructions. When after a time nothing had happened he wrote again. He wrote repeatedly. These were matters of great concern to him; they dealt with corruption in the Church, they also dealt with people's rights, something he had fought for all his life. Sadly, at Leominster, he lost the fight. Ironically it was his adversary, Archbishop Pecham, who achieved a solution.[8] After visiting the Priory, Pecham paid for the building of a chapel, known as the Forbury Chapel, between the priory and the town for the use of the parishioners. How bitter for Thomas that the man who caused his downfall should have solved the problem he had battled with so long. Though, perhaps, being Thomas, he would simply have been glad for the sake of the Church – had he known. The chapel was completed in 1284; he had died two years before.

CHAPTER IX

In April 1278 came unexpected news. Archbishop Kilwardby was to be made a cardinal. This was most unusual. A Dominican, an English friar? Admittedly Kilwardby would not have been the first; there had even been one Dominican Pope, Innocent V, in 1276, but Dominican cardinals were generally rare. There must have been murmurings within the Church, speculation, the shaking of heads. Did Pope Nicholas III consider it was time for a change? Had the Archbishop proved unsatisfactory? Could the strain of his office have proved too much?

Whatever the reason, or fusion of reasons, Kilwardby must have found his role difficult. He was a friar, a scholar, a metaphysical thinker. As archbishop his time was spent largely on administration, on financial matters, particularly the crusading tax. This punitive tax had been imposed by Pope Gregory X, at the second Council of Lyons in 1274, and was the cause of much resentment in the Church. Kilwardby was caught unhappily between his duty to obey the Pope and sympathy towards his clergy who particularly objected to the interference of the papal legate. This increasingly fraught situation must have made the thought of escaping to Rome seem to Kilwardby like a peaceful dream. He left with few regrets, taking with him a quantity of treasures belonging to the Church; books, manuscripts, ornaments, registers.

Heads may well have shaken over that as well.

Thomas must have been sad at the leaving of the man who was probably his oldest and dearest friend. Possibly, too, he felt a touch of apprehension at the news of his successor. It was John Pecham.

Thomas had known the new archbishop for many years. In Paris when he had returned there after Evesham to study theology, Pecham had been one of his masters. He still spoke of Thomas as his student; there was no outward animosity. But, faced with Thomas's courtly reserve, his air of austerity and gravitas, it may be that Pecham's self-importance grew more pronounced so that an earlier impression Thomas had of him had been reinforced. That had come from an incident in Paris when Pecham, brash and over-assertive had been cut down to size by Thomas Aquinas. Thomas would not have forgotten that.

But if Pecham was garrulous and overbearing, and had a reputation for being so, he could also be friendly and forthcoming; he spoke his mind openly, often tactlessly, but at least people knew where they stood with him. He was zealous, energetic; he had boundless drive, he made a lot of noise. He was about as different from Thomas in character as it was possible to be. They were incompatible. As Sir Maurice Powicke puts it, they were oil and water; the chemistry was wrong.[1] And perhaps already, from their slight acquaintance, each of them had sensed it, had felt the vibrations in the air ...

In the last few years, with Thomas at Hereford and Pecham at Oxford, then, briefly, in Rome, they would have managed to avoid each other. But following Pecham's consecration in February 1279, they would have met not only at episcopal gatherings but also at parliaments and government councils, for Pecham, as Archbishop and therefore a tenant-in-chief of the King, was automatically a member of the Great Council. At all such meetings they would have greeted each other quite amiably; there was no reason, after all, to do otherwise.

Pecham, typically, got to grips with his new role immediately, summoning the bishops to a meeting at Reading in July. Its main purpose was to enforce the reforms set out at the second Council of Lyons with an important addition, the ending of pluralism. This could have put Thomas, a renowned pluralist, in an awkward position, for though he had fought against the abuse of pluralism, he could scarcely claim to be against it altogether. And while, unlike Walter Cantilupe, he may not have gone as far as actually advocating the practice, the issue is likely to have put him on the defensive at Reading. Indeed, as T. F. Tout points out, he took the lead in opposing Pecham's more controversial policies. The new archbishop's bustling and officious manner, his attempts to push through reforms that appeared either too radical or unworkable, won Thomas the backing of many of his fellow bishops. The points of difference were drawn up in twenty-one articles, which were presented to Pecham early in 1282, by which time his forceful tactics over a number of issues had made him yet more unpopular. In the meantime he had thought out a plan to end pluralism, such a heavily organized and detailed plan, with an army of agents recruited to collect evidence, that it could not fail, or so Pecham believed. But the agents met resistance and evasion. Pluralism was deep-rooted. With wealthy landowners controlling the entitlement of numerous livings the practice was built into the feudal life of the countryside. In any case, papal dispensation, a guaranteed let-out, continued to be easily obtained.

Soon after the Reading Council Thomas made preparations to go abroad. According to the patent rolls for August 1279 he procured letters of protection and safe conduct, a regular requirement when travelling overseas, furthermore his register includes a number of entries, dated 12th September and 19th September, noting the appointment of various officials who were to act for him 'during his absence in foreign parts.'

Why did he plan to go away? Why, having got as far as Kent – there are letters in the register sent from Ightham – did he change his mind and turn back? Had he planned to visit his dear friend Robert Kilwardby and then, at the last minute, heard of his unexpected death at Viterbo? Had something happened at the Reading Council, possibly a sharp exchange with Pecham, that made him decide to leave England for a while? Was it his aim to avoid Pecham's enthronement on 8th October? Did he then decide it was his duty to be there?

But whether he made it to Pecham's enthronement, to what must have been a most splendid occasion, a great social event attended by all the most powerful, is doubtful. For, according to the register, on 7th October he sent a present of an altar frontal to Matthew, the Cardinal from Whaddon. Whaddon, a chapelry close to Morton in Worcestershire, was four or five days' ride away from Canterbury. What's more in another letter sent on 11th October, Thomas expresses his regret that he cannot take part in discussions with 'the Primate and his Suffragans' owing to illness.

Thomas was over sixty now and, it must be true that for several reasons his health was starting to deteriorate. Not only did he fast according to the church calendar – the feasts of the Virgin Mary were particularly important to him – he regularly existed on the most meagre diet.[2] On one occasion Robert of Gloucester exclaimed at Thomas's abstinence, 'You eat and drink too little, my lord. You will not be able to last out.' When there was no response Robert tried again and was told to hold his tongue and leave his master in peace. But, Thomas added, Robert should please himself, eating and drinking whatever he liked. Another time when William de Montfort, Dean of Saint Paul's, warning Thomas that to eat so little would weaken his health, asked how he would have the strength to 'venture on such arduous enterprise as his suits with Pecham and the Earl of Gloucester?' Thomas answered the Dean by asking him not to watch what he ate and drank; furthermore, as a priest, the Dean must not reveal until after Thomas's death, that for the past thirty-two years he had not risen from the table without feeling as hungry as when he sat down. Yet he insisted, and perhaps he smiled, he was strong enough to 'venture on a battle with you.'

A story[3] is told of how Robert Grosseteste once advised a Dominican priest that the three things essential to temporal salvation were food, sleep and good humour. On another occasion he is said to have ordered a gloomy friar to drink a cup of the best wine. Had such a highly respected figure ordered Thomas to do so, would he have obeyed? Almost certainly not. His abstinence was a kind of penance; he did it for God; to have relented, even briefly, would have seemed a betrayal, despite the fact that, as he must have known, such an inadequate diet was affecting his health, possibly irreparably.

Another penance he had practised for many years was the wearing of a hair shirt. It was a particular garment he had inherited from his uncle, Walter Cantilupe, who had died in 1266. At the canonization hearings Robert of Gloucester explained that Thomas had considered the shirt was not harsh enough so had sent it to Oxford for roughening and hardening. Walter Cantilupe also left him a hair belt which Thomas wore at night, hiding it under the bedclothes during the day, where it was eventually discovered by Hugh le Barber. In his testimony Hugh described how every morning he found lice all over his master's bedding, his clothing, even inside his boots. There were so many lice Hugh could never manage to get rid of them and each day he found more, a verminous, writhing mass of them, lice *ad abhominationem*. He could not understand it. Roger de Kirketon, the secretary, told him that some men had lice naturally, but one day while at Oxford, when Thomas was at the schools, Hugh found something strange between the sheets. It was a belt made of grey coloured hair, 'two hands breadth, knotty and spiky' and alive, *tota repleta*, with lice. The only way he could clean it was with a sharp point (of a knife). He then laid it beneath the foot of the bed. Later, Hugh said that Roger had questioned him about finding the belt, and then made him vow to speak of it to no one, for Thomas had been most concerned at its discovery.

Thomas worked at full stretch throughout the day, and, according to Hugh le Barber, he always studied until late, rising before dawn to say the 'hours'.[4] Which left little time for much needed sleep, Grosseteste's second necessity for temporal salvation. And once in bed how much did Thomas sleep? How much could he sleep with the constant irritation of squirming lice between the hairy spikes that encircled him?

And the third of Grosseteste's necessities, good humour? Thomas was said to be sociable; he was famously hospitable and doubtless appreciated good conversation. But he was of a serious nature, learned and intelligent; it is hard to imagine him bursting into laughter, or laughing at all. Quiet good humour was more his style.

There was little good humour in his dealings with Pecham. It was early in 1280 that their conflict began, a drama in which they were the principal players with a plot given substance by their chemistry, the oil and water of their characters. The first cause of trouble was a matrimonial dispute between Petronilla Bebler and Richard de Bamford, which was heard in the Dean's Court in Hereford by the subdean, not the dean himself. The subdean found against Richard de Bamford who decided to bypass the usual intermediate procedure, an appeal to the Hereford Bishop's Consistory Court, and appeal directly to the Court of Arches. This was the Consistory Court of Canterbury, which dealt with the administration of ecclesiastical law and which met in the vestry of Saint Mary-le-Bow in Cheapside.[5] Next the subdean received a letter from an official at Canterbury prohibiting him from carrying out his adjudication, and, in the version told by Canon Capes, fining him ten marks. Angrily flinging the letter in the mud, he had Richard de Bamford and his agent arrested on the spot. An order was then despatched to Thomas instructing him to excommunicate the subdean. Failure to do so, he was informed, would result in suspension from his chapel with an interdict, an exclusion, from taking part in all ecclesiastical matters, a deeply serious and disproportionate threat. Canon Capes claims that, at that stage, Pecham was taking no active part in this vitriolic exchange as it is not mentioned in his register. No active part. But if that is true, he must surely have known what was going on and made no attempt to prevent it. Thomas doubtless suspected so. He stood his ground, refusing to excommunicate his subdean. He believed the whole case should have come under his own jurisdiction from the start.

And then there was a long interval. Thomas went away, left the country – he really did this time. In July 1280 he summoned his clergy to explain to them his disagreement with Pecham and to ask them for help with travelling expenses. This they did, and generously, contributing about one hundred pounds, though it took a while to arrive and Thomas was not prepared to wait. Two letters in the register, dated 25th July, instruct his official to pay all monies from all sources to his temporary treasurer, Nicholas the Penitentiary, who is requested to send the money on. In the meantime, having put Robert of Gloucester, recently appointed Chancellor of Hereford, in charge of the diocese, Thomas set off across the channel to Normandy. He headed for Breteuil, a region he knew well, where the parish of Evreux had links with his mother's family. He took lodgings, and, Canon Capes tells us, was warmly welcomed at the Benedictine Abbey of Lyre, where the abbot held a canonry of

Hereford Cathedral. The monastery had been built two centuries before by William FitzOsbern, the first Earl of Hereford. Since then the monastery had prospered and expanded till, in Thomas's time, it housed forty to fifty monks who made a good living from the fertile land. The countryside was gentle and peaceful with the river Risle winding through the valley. After the troubles at Hereford, Thomas must have welcomed some time apart, time to unwind and meditate.

It was probably while he was staying at Lyre, that he brought an apparently drowned child back to life. There are different versions of the story but the most detailed claims that a three-year-old child had fallen into the fast-flowing Risle, which ran close to the abbey gates. Thomas came upon the parents, who, having pulled their child out of the water, were crouching in despair over the small lifeless body lying on the bank. He comforted them, reassuring them, that with God's help, their child would live. Making the sign of the cross, he inserted the father's knife into the child's mouth, tilting the body so that water drained out. Then, quickly carrying the child's body to the monastery, he held it close to a fire, while the parents chafed the body with their hands, warming it and warming it until, at last there was movement, slight at first, an intake of breath … Life had returned. A miracle.

It was not till several years after his death, when the parents of the child heard about Saint Thomas of Hereford, that they realized the identity of the unknown priest who had brought their drowned child back to life.

Thomas was in Normandy for about a year. Why he stayed so long, abandoning his diocese is unexplained; it seems somehow out of character. Perhaps it had something to do with a possible appeal over his dispute with Pecham and the fact that from July 1280 for several months, there was no pope to appeal to. While in Normandy he is thought to have spent some time travelling round the region, stopping in small villages. In two such places, Argentan and Lisieux, ancient relics, still on display – a comb at Argentan, vestments at Lisieux – are attributed to Thomas of Canterbury. There is no evidence that Becket ever visited either place. It is now believed they belonged to Thomas of Hereford.[6]

In the early autumn of 1281 Thomas went home, stopping en route in Canterbury where he called on Pecham. The meeting was, if not exactly friendly, at least not openly hostile. Perhaps Thomas had not yet heard that while he was away Robert of Gloucester had been receiving various mandates intended for Thomas, hostile orders against which he had appealed to the papal court. Thomas soon found himself bombarded by a repeat of these mandates and in October he also appealed to the papal court.

The cause of this latest trouble concerned the property of Henry de Hawkley, a Canon of Hereford, who had recently died. Henry de Hawkley's property turned out to be in more than one diocese, in which case, said Pecham, it was he who, as Archbishop, should have jurisdiction over the probate. Robert of Gloucester rejected Pecham's claim. Pecham, once again, over-reacted, ordering Thomas to excommunicate Robert of Gloucester. Predictably Thomas refused, informing Pecham that an appeal about the case had already been sent to the papal court.

Thomas and Pecham did not come face to face until early February 1282. Through the darkest weeks of winter Thomas stayed in the diocese, spending Christmas at Bishop's Castle, moving on to Wigmore Abbey for New Year. Throughout that time more and more letters arrived from Pecham ordering him to deal with Robert of Gloucester. To each one Thomas replied, politely and with dignity, refusing to give in; the matter was being considered at Rome. Pecham then wrote warning him that he was under sentence of excommunication, but that if he would agree to punish Robert of Gloucester, the sentence would be withdrawn. In a letter dated 7th January, recorded in Pecham's register, Thomas replied that he would not change his mind, Pecham's offer was unacceptable. A week later he sent his clerk Robert Wych with Hildebrand, the notary, to the Court of Arches to appeal against Robert of Gloucester's sentence. At once, Pecham dispatched letters to his proctors at the papal court warning them to watch those representing Thomas; at the same time requesting the help of various cardinals, making sure he had their support.

From Wigmore Thomas moved to Bosbury and then slowly made his way to London, to Lambeth Palace, where Pecham had summoned all his bishops to attend a conference on 3rd February. Thomas took part in the conference, joining in the four days of general discussion, during which he and Pecham managed to avoid outright fireworks, though word that letters from Rome had arrived for Thomas, which he emphatically denied, must have raised the temperature a bit.

It was after the conference was over, when on the morning of Saturday 7th February, Thomas met Pecham at Lambeth Palace with the aim of discussing their differences, that matters came to a head. Accounts of the meeting are found in the sworn testimony of a number of witnesses at the canonization hearings, but, as these were given twenty-five years after the event, they vary a good deal and are fairly confused. However recent research by the historian, R. C. Finucane, into the mass of documentation relating to the whole dispute, has greatly added to what was previously known, filling in the gaps and making it possible to picture the scene with those taking part, the members of the cast and the roles they played.[7]

The actors were seated at a long table under the south-facing window in the great hall, Thomas and Pecham probably opposite each other, with their officials on either side of them. The two principals, the leading players, stood out in marked contrast; Thomas, straight-backed, patrician, with a stillness about him, an impression of calm, or perhaps of emotion tightly controlled yet increasingly detectable; and Pecham, dynamic, vociferous, jabbing a finger to make a point, thumping his fist, then leaning to listen, head poked forward, quick to interrupt, raising his voice to disagree.

The opening statements, setting out the situation, were probably reasonably matter of fact. That businesslike atmosphere soon changed for, at some point in the early stages, Thomas was handed a repeat of the order to excommunicate Robert of Gloucester. Immediately backs stiffened, the tension rose, discussion turned to argument then to anger, harsh voices filling the hall. Suddenly Pecham, leaping to his feet, charged across to the door of a small adjoining room, flung it open and disappeared. His party hastily followed. The door slammed shut.

Thomas and his men must have breathed deep breaths, mopped their foreheads, eyeing each other as muffled talk sounded through the door.

126

Inside the small room Pecham, still at boiling point, at once ordered Beccles, his notary, to write out a notice of excommunication on Thomas, Bishop of Hereford. That is according to one account. In another version, that told by John de Lewes, who was with Pecham in the room, there was further discussion before they all came to a joint decision. He also described how as Pecham instructed Robert de Lacy, one of his advisers, to go back into the hall and read out the order of excommunication, his eyes filled with tears. We know Robert de Lacy followed these instructions but whether, as he and John de Lewes testified in 1307, he came right into the hall and sat facing Thomas to read out the order, or whether, as members of Thomas's party maintained, he stood in the doorway reading from a small piece of parchment something that nobody could hear, is not clear at all. Another ambiguity is the wording of the order. Pecham's register states 'if you do not obey our warnings henceforth we excommunicate you'. Was this another warning or a valid sentence?

These were the questions anxiously debated by Thomas and his people inside the hall. But what they needed was to study the document. One of them, possibly Thomas himself, went to the door and demanded a copy. Nothing happened. When, three hours later, still nothing had happened, according to the notary, Hildebrand, Thomas went to the door again, banged it with his fist and shouted that he intended to appeal to the Pope, adding that, out of reverence to the Apostolic See, Pecham should listen to him. While he was speaking the door opened a little way, then slammed shut in his face, which he asked everyone present to note. Robert Wych maintained that Thomas's foot was caught in the door causing him to limp back to the bench. Whether true or not it must have been more than his foot that ached as he and his party made their way wearily out of the hall. But before they left Thomas instructed his scribe to write out a copy of his appeal to the Pope which eventually was handed to one of Pecham's officials who emerged from the room. For, tired and wrung out though he must have been, Thomas had no thought of a breathing space, of taking time to rest, and, having crossed the Thames to his London house, he spent the rest of the day consulting his advisers and the many wise and experienced friends who called to find out how he had fared and then joined the discussion, staying late into the night, talking earnestly by candle-light.

First Thomas was concerned to establish whether it was right to carry on. Was his cause just? Or should he give up? The answers, unquestionably 'yes' to the first and 'no' to the second, must have been what he hoped to hear and he readily agreed to carry on, vowing that he would fight *usque ad mortem*, to the death. This would later be seen as a prophetic statement. It could also be seen as dogged perseverance, as stubbornness. He had never given in; he never would. Pecham was to accuse him of 'obdurate contumacy'. Stubbornness was a quality they shared, probably the only one.

That evening with the help of his advisers, he mapped out his campaign. First and foremost he made the dramatic decision to go to Rome himself and to set out as soon as possible.

He wrote at once to the King requesting leave to go abroad, at the same time asking for his support. Records show that Edward responded immediately, for a week later he sent a letter from Sherborne in support of Thomas to Cardinal Matthew Rosso Orsini. Letters of protection and safe conduct to the court of Rome arrived two days later.

Before Thomas set off there were important matters to deal with. One was to prepare the case he would present to the papal Curia; another was to fortify his position at home. On both these counts he probably relied more than anyone on the papal collector and chaplain, Master Ardicio de Comite, who, as a canon of Hereford, had been with him at the Lambeth meeting. Ardicio knew canon law, he knew the workings of the Curia, he also had friends at Rome; he was thus able to lobby for Thomas both at home and at the Curia. He was insistent, however, that Thomas's immediate concern should be to clarify his position with Pecham. It was essential that Pecham should hear the appeal he had tried to make at Lambeth read aloud.

Thomas chose his clerk, Robert Wych, to carry this out. Or, possibly, Robert Wych, energetic and zealous, volunteered. He set off at once heading for Mortlake, where Pecham had gone from Lambeth Palace. But on 9th February Robert found that Pecham had left Mortlake and was travelling to Guildford. Putting on speed he caught up with Pecham's party on the road near the priory of Newark, where they had stopped to rest. Robert tried to explain who he was, and to read out the appeal. Pecham would not listen. Riding on he ordered his retainers to get rid of 'this rascal ... because he was excommunicated'. Robert was seized and thrown into the ditch by the side of the road. According to a witness the ditch was full, the water was filthy and icy cold. Nonetheless Robert followed, perhaps after a pause at the nearby priory to dry his clothes, and the next day at Guildford, though barred from seeing Pecham, he was able to meet some of Pecham's officials in the parish church and hand over the appeal. From that moment Pecham can have had no doubt of Thomas's refusal to accept his earlier ruling. There was no question now of a conditional sentence. The excommunication was fact.

On 11th February Thomas moved to Earley near Reading, then, a few days later on to Prestbury in Worcestershire. Though not accompanying him, Ardicio kept Thomas up to date on the numerous letters he fired off to Rome, to the Bishop of London and to other bishops. On 17th February Pecham had written to all the bishops explaining Thomas's behaviour and the resulting sentence. He instructed the Bishop of London, Richard Gravesend, to publish the excommunication within the next three months, the understanding being there was no hurry. He clearly was unaware of Thomas's plan to go to Rome.

Ardicio, who seems to have relished this war of words, immediately followed Pecham's letters to the bishops by writing to all of them again, setting out his own version of events. He insisted that, since appeals to the Curia had already been made, the sentence was unjust, that it had been issued without proper warning, in the heat of the moment, when the archbishop had been 'moved by rancour of spirit'. Writing to Thomas with a copy of his letter to the Curia, Ardicio added that 'Philip' was on his way to the papal court to discuss matters with the Hereford proctors there. (Philip was almost certainly Philip de Comite, a nephew of Ardicio, whose appointment in August 1280 to the prebend of Inkberrow in the Hereford diocese is recorded in the register.)

Ardicio next advised Thomas to take a copy of his

appeal first to the Bishop of London, then to all other bishops. He must convince them he was in the right, that he needed their support. In fact since the Reading conference when Thomas had led the opposition to Pecham's reforms, he felt confident he could count on the support of a number of bishops. But by no means all. If he could not win the backing of the opposition at least he must aim for their neutrality.

To visit every bishop in the land, to persuade them to comply with his request, was asking a good deal of anyone. Thomas again asked Robert Wych.

On 6th March, armed with copies of the letters and statements, Robert set off. With him went Hildebrand, the notary, who kept a written account of their expedition. On Ardicio's advice they began with the Bishop of London, then, as it was nearby, Roger bravely decided to try once again to read out Thomas's appeal in the Court of Arches.

Arriving at Bow Church Robert asked the dean, Roger de Rothwell, if he might read something aloud to him. The dean readily agreed but after a few words, realizing what it was about, he interrupted. He was too busy to listen at the moment, he said; Robert should go into some corner of the church and read it there. Robert, refusing to be put off, started again, reading *velociter*, at top speed. He did not get far. The dean, astonished by such insolence, *mirabiliter est turbatus*, ordered three of his men to throw Robert out immediately. Robert, seized by the arms, continued to read while others who were there, supporters of Thomas, battled to free him. The dean, highly incensed, forbade everyone there to listen to Robert, threatening them with excommunication should they do so. And out they all scuttled, leaving Robert to read the rest of the appeal to an empty court.

A week later Pecham, having heard of Thomas's imminent departure, wrote urgently to the Bishop of London, instructing him to excommunicate Thomas by 30th March. At the same time he wrote to the Dean of the Arches, asking him to publish the sentence in every London church by 30th March, because the Bishop of London had failed as yet to do so, a rather unfair allegation it would seem. The Dean of the Arches must have been delighted to comply.

Robert Wych and Hildebrand continued to travel from bishop to bishop. It took them six weeks to complete their mission, six weeks of hard travelling, of persistent campaigning in a sometimes hostile atmosphere. Their low point came at Exeter, where having called on the bishop, they learned that Pecham was due to arrive there next day. Robert, valiant as ever, approached Pecham in the cathedral and, asking him to listen, began to read out Thomas's appeal. Pecham furious, *irato animo*, refused, ordering Robert to leave at once. Robert continued to read, ignoring Pecham who was shouting at his men to throw Robert out. And this time they did, seizing him and dragging him through the cathedral while Pecham watched and Robert yelled over his shoulder, protesting that the men were maltreating him. When Pecham then ordered his release, Robert stood at the door of the chapter house, where Pecham had retreated, and bellowed the appeal at the top of his voice.

The incident ended with the archdeacon inviting Robert to read whatever he wished in the cathedral, promising to listen on behalf of the Archbishop. Which, perhaps rather hoarsely, Robert did.

CHAPTER X

On Monday 9th March 1282, Thomas began his most momentous journey. He had travelled all his life, in England and on the Continent. This time was different. On the outcome of this journey, its success or failure, much depended, not only his own future, but its effect on the Hereford diocese, on the reputation of the church, its probity, or lack of it. He would surely have thought of it in that way, seen his journey as a mission, a crusade in the cause of justice and human rights. The significance of the whole undertaking must have weighed heavily on his mind. So much could go wrong, on the journey, on arrival. How ardently he must have prayed all would be well.

The journey did go reasonably well. At least there were no major disasters, as far as we know. And, owing to a remarkable discovery, what might truly be called serendipity, we do know a good deal about it all.

In 1998, Rosalind Caird, the Hereford Cathedral archivist, unearthed a collection of unidentified medieval account rolls. Amongst them was one that turned out to be the expense account for Thomas's journey from London to the papal court in Italy. From this long strip of parchment,[1] the original document, written in a hand typical of the Edwardian period[2] we can learn the names of the towns where Thomas and his retinue found lodgings, we can chart their route, find that while they followed the rivers, they mainly chose roads – the rutted tracks that passed as roads – that ran above the valley bottoms. In Italy they followed the coastal roads avoiding the treacherous mountain route. Even so the heaviest baggage was sent by sea for spring rains brought the risk of flooded roads, of the waggons and horses getting stuck in heavy mud; possibly they did. For, while they averaged twenty miles a day it was sometimes considerably less.

The household roll states the expenditure for each day, with the total for the week, from Sunday to Saturday. Sundays are identified by being the nearest before or after the feast day of a particular saint. The first Sunday, the day before they set off from London, was the nearest before Saint Gregory's Feast Day, 12th March, when the expenses came to 47s 3d. Possibly this enormous sum, the equivalent of roughly £12,000 today, was spent mainly on provisions for the journey. In contrast the bill for Tuesday of that week, when they stopped for the night at Eastham in Essex, came to just over 15s. For Friday, when they stayed the night at Dover, the bill was 30s 2d. By the time they reached Boulogne on Saturday expenditure for the week added up to £12 9s 7d. When you consider that the annual wage for a priest was between £3 and £4, it hardly seems that Thomas was trying to economize despite the heavy debts hanging over him.

For the next eight weeks as the party travelled

through France and Italy the bills appear astounding; over 100s for Monday 13th April, when they spent the night at Nimes, while the total for that week was £28 11s 10¹/₂d. However these figures are deceptive for they have been converted by Thomas's accountants to the sterling equivalent of the French Tournois, the regional currency, which was of lower value than LSD sterling. During the journey Thomas and his party passed through eleven different currency zones, in some of which, particularly in Italy, the regional currency was markedly weaker than the strong and stable LSD sterling. As Rosalind Caird points out, there was surely a far more convincing case for the euro in 1282 than there is today.

Reaching Paris on 21st March, Thomas decided to stay there a few days. In this city he knew well there was the opportunity to see old friends, to seek their advice, and to catch up with his correspondence. From Paris he wrote to Richard Gravesend, Bishop of London, explaining the circumstances of his case and asking him not to publish the excommunication. He enclosed letters he had received from the Curia some time earlier, adding the suggestion that the whole matter be discussed at the Easter council.

Ten days later, when Thomas, having crossed the Loire was approaching Nevers, Pecham was sending further instructions to his curial proctors warning them of rumours that Thomas himself was on his way to the Curia. He, Pecham, had heard nothing of this. However, should such stories prove true, Thomas must be travelling secretly, *sed occulte*, and by the most devious routes, twisting and weaving with the cunning of a fox. The proctors should resist him strenuously when he arrived – if, indeed, he did – for he was the chief obstacle to Pecham's business, being crafty and 'in all actions false'. It was in this letter that Pecham famously described Thomas as a man who 'excogitated malice under the demeanour of a dove'.[3]

This long message, sent on 31st March, would have allowed time for Thomas's letter from Paris to have reached Richard Gravesend, and for him to have discussed it with his fellow bishops. Murmurings of this may then have filtered through to Pecham, spurring him to write to his proctors. And possibly the tone of his letter, its self-righteousness, its vitriolic references to Thomas, was because he felt the opposition gaining strength. Which may well have been so. His high-handed reaction to the twenty-one articles criticizing his reforms had caused resentment among many bishops; Pecham, it was said, had behaved as if he was royalty. And now there was his feud with Thomas Cantilupe, pursued with an almost maniacal zeal. Where would it end?

For good measure, and perhaps to emphasize his authority, Pecham announced the formal excommunication of Robert Wych. Robert, who had expected this anyway, set off to join Thomas in early May bringing letters of support. And at that time of year when, with luck the roads were dry, riding at speed, as, knowing the importance of the letters to Thomas Robert would have done, he most likely arrived in early June. Though generally the journey took between five and seven weeks, it was possible to reach Italy from England in twenty-five days. It must have cheered Thomas to have him there.

Thomas needed cheering, for by the time Robert caught up with him, things were not going well. Thomas was ill. This had first been reported when the party reached Florence on 14th May. Unable to go on,

Thomas sent two of his senior clergy, Robert de Radeswell and John de Kempsey, with a layman, Richard Cissor, ahead of him to the Curia.

At that time both the papal court and the Curia had moved from Rome, which was caught up in serious political troubles, to a more peaceful papal residence at Orvieto. The turbulent state of Italian affairs was to last for many years culminating eventually in the removal of the papal court to Avignon.

When Robert de Radeswell and his companions arrived in Orvieto they found that Pecham's proctors had put it about that Thomas, as an excommunicate, was unfit to appear at the Curia. For Thomas, lying ill in Florence, this was discouraging news. But Radeswell at once got hold of the renowned Italian scholar, Master Angelus, who with Thomas's proctors, John of Bitterley, and the prestigious, Adam of Fileby, called on the cardinals.[4] The cardinals listened sympathetically, then advised the proctors to petition the Pope. After repeated *peticionem*, two eminent cardinals, Benedict Gaetani, later Pope Boniface VIII, and John Chioletti,[5] were appointed to investigate the case.

The two *auditories* with a number of assistant cardinals met the opposing proctors in the hall of the papal palace to examine the letters of authorization and to hear both sides. But this august body in their scarlet robes were clearly unimpressed by the scant evidence produced by Pecham's proctors. Indeed, testifying at the canonization hearings, Radeswell describes one of the assisting cardinals, Matthew Rosso, as smiling, *subridendo*, (sardonically?), as he asked Pecham's proctors for further proof that Thomas was not a man of proper condition. It was Matthew Rosso to whom Edward had written on Thomas's behalf in February.

More letters were produced, which added little to the evidence and, though the hearings went on, they were largely inconclusive. Eventually in the first week of June, the cardinals pronounced 'that good man the Bishop of Hereford to be a man of fit and proper status and, as such, he ought to be admitted' to the Curia.[6]

John of Bitterly wrote to tell Thomas the good news and at once Radeswell rode off at top speed to deliver the letter to Thomas's new lodgings south of Florence. Soon afterwards, probably on 9th June, Thomas met Radeswell at a village close to Orvieto to hear about the meetings at the Curia. Thomas had recovered from his illness in Florence, partially at least, and talking to Radeswell must have lifted his spirits and given him hope. In the morning they travelled on together to Orvieto.

Thomas was greeted by the cardinals and by Pope Martin IV. All of them were warm and welcoming. And there at his lodgings Thomas found presents from the Pope, a brace of capons set on silver dishes, two vessels of wine. And, after a sample tasting by the messenger, who was given half a mark, Thomas and his party sat down to eat. All of which, however little Thomas ate himself, was further encouragement, further hope. He must have felt that the Pope was on his side.

A few days later he visited Pope Martin at his palace. Martin IV, Simon de Brie, who came from Touraine, was said to be mild and indecisive. His elevation to pope in 1281, against his will, was due to the influence of Charles of Anjou, the powerful King of Sicily, who continued to control him politically. He was Charles's puppet; Charles pulled the strings. Having reinstated Charles as a Roman senator,

Martin succeeded in destroying the unity of the Latin and Greek churches achieved at the Council of Lyons in 1274 by excommunicating the Byzantine Emperor. As a result he was hated by the Romans and, taking no chances, he never set foot in Rome as Pope.

The fact that Charles of Anjou knew Edward well proved useful to Thomas, for in February, at the start of the dispute, Edward had written to Cardinal Rosso on Thomas's behalf. Matthew Rosso would have brought this to the notice of the Pope.

Politics apart, Pope Martin was kind-hearted, a compassionate man. Thomas's appearance clearly concerned him; the English bishop was haggard and painfully thin. Martin is known to have lived well, enjoying his food. He had a particular fondness for eels from the nearby Lake Bolsena cooked in vernaccia, the golden wine of Tuscany and Lazio. Indeed, according to one story, he is said to have died of indigestion caused by a surfeit of local eels. Once upon a time he and Thomas could have compared the merits of eel and lamprey, but not any more. Thomas had denied himself too long to remember the taste of his favourite dish. Eyeing him that day, Pope Martin suggested he sit down on his own bed, which Thomas did most gratefully. Why, asked Pope Martin, had Thomas had not come to see him more often? He had heard that the doorkeepers had not allowed him in.

Thomas had been prepared for this possibility. He knew all about oiling the wheels with hand-outs to influential cardinals. A year before, according to his register, he had instructed his curial proctors to distribute one hundred pounds in gifts to 'expedite his affairs at Rome', and his accounts show that while in Orvieto another sixty-three pounds was spent for the same purpose. That day, however, discreetly bypassing Pope Martin's remark, he said, 'Holy Father, I have been worn out, and still am'.[7]

It was sadly true. He was worn out from the journey, from his recent illness, from the strain of worry over legal disputes, worries that had been with him for several years. The case against the Bishop of Saint Asaph was still dragging on, and then there was conflict with Peter de Langon, who had recently stepped up his action over the prebend of Hereford. Most of all the feud with Pecham worried him. Pope Martin's welcome was encouraging. Yet, at this stage, who could tell how the dice would fall? The workings of the Curia were deep and strange and notoriously slow. Rumours from London – and they were surely no more than that – suggesting the bishops had reached agreement with Pecham over their differences concerning jurisdiction at the Easter council so that Thomas could now safely return, were hard to believe. Even more so the message from the Bishop of Norwich sent off at the end of April, assuring him that Pecham had suspended all action against him. Why, in that case was Pecham still firing off letters to his proctors in terms so vindictive that Cardinal Gaetano wrote advising the Archbishop to tone down abusive language. Pecham, clearly stung, replied self-righteously how surprised and saddened he was to learn that Gaetano had been duped by Thomas, his honeyed lips, his false piety. Could the Cardinal not see that Thomas had acted in the spirit of Dathan and Abyron, who rose against Moses and were swallowed up by the earth?

In late June or early July Pope Martin with his court moved the short distance from Orvieto to Montefiascone, the chief papal residence in Tuscany. On 4th

July Thomas and his household followed them to Ferento, about ten kilometres away. Their lodgings at the Castrum Florenti, now a ruin, were cramped and ill-equipped and the household account shows that nearly six pounds had to be spent on bedding. Throughout July Thomas travelled to the Curia two or three times a week to listen to the hearings of his case. Then at the beginning of August, while the appeals and petitions were still being considered, he fell ill again. This time the illness was more serious. Canon Capes suggests malaria, high fever, 'aggravated internal disorders'. Richard Strange writes of 'his crazy body worn out with former labours ... destitute for victuals'. He was nursed with great care by the servants who were closest and most fond of him. Of these it was probably Robert Deynte, who had looked after him for fifteen years, who knew him most intimately, who understood him and loved him best.

On 14th August Pope Martin came to the Castrum Florenti to see Thomas. With him was the faithful Robert Wych. Perhaps they could tell this would be goodbye.

Somehow on the 16th and 17th August Thomas managed to celebrate Mass. It was the last time he did so. Each day he grew visibly weaker. Visitors calling at the Castrum Florenti anxious for news, must have doubted his chance of recovery. His servants attending him devotedly – Robert Deynte was with him night and day – must have felt the same. The doctor advised clysters – enemas – a horrible indignity, though possibly Thomas was too ill to mind. Yet it seemed he did not lose consciousness, for in the last week of his life, having been given permission by Pope Martin, he made a will.[8] And despite his weakness he thought it all out most carefully, matching legacies to individuals.

No copy has survived but the notary who drew it up, most likely an Italian, wrote out receipts of legacies given to members of Thomas's household. There were bequests of money, generous sums; there were horses, mules, cloaks. Robert Wych received twenty marks, a furred cloak with a hood, a piece of white cloth and a horse called Asshe. Robert Deynte was also left twenty marks. John de Clare, Thomas's agent, who was chosen to run the household, would have forty marks, a mule and a piece of dark blue cloth.

The will completed, he was given absolution by a papal penitentiary. This was later to prove an important factor in the consideration of his sanctity. Afterwards, perhaps, he felt he could let go, he no longer had to fight for recovery, he was ready to die. Outwardly, it seems, there was little change.

It was the evening of Tuesday 25th August, when it was starting to grow dark, when the household had retired to their rooms and only Nicholas, the chaplain, and the servant who looked after the wardrobe, were there, in the chamber, with Robert Deynte. Perhaps there was a sign, a change in Thomas's breathing, a rattle in his chest. The three of them drew closer, hovered round the bed, watching in the fading light. It was Robert who knew the time had come, who took Thomas in his arms. They heard him murmur faintly, 'I commend my spirit.'

Moments afterwards he died.

CHAPTER XI

The body of Thomas Cantilupe lay exposed for six days emanating a heavenly fragrance.'

Though the words of Richard Strange sound over-euphemistic, they in fact reflect the popular belief in what was known as 'the odour of sanctity' said to surround the body of a saint. It was, as the late Dean of Hereford, Norman Rathbone, described it, a sensible sign of the supernatural sweetness of their soul.

After six days, or perhaps rather sooner in the August heat, the body was prepared for the funeral. In accordance with medieval practice, the heart was removed and the flesh separated from the bones. (Generally the bones were boiled, preserving and tending to discolour them.)

The funeral took place at the monastery of San Severo, the house of an order of Premonstratensian canons. The fact that no less than five cardinals were there – unwelcome news for Pecham when he heard of it – indicates the respect Thomas had earned. For the members of Thomas's household and for Robert

Wych, all of whom were there, the occasion must have been deeply moving. The Requiem Mass was celebrated by the Franciscan Cardinal Jerome of Oporto, who in 1288 became Pope Nicholas IV. Following his sermon, a long eulogy on the life of Thomas, came the interment of the casket containing the flesh. The exact spot, according to those who were there, was close to the south door leading to the cloisters.

Afterwards, emerging from the shadowed church into the glaring sunlight, the members of the household made their way back to the Castrum Florenti to pack up their belongings for the long trek home. It would have touched them that, as Thomas lay dying, he had thought of their needs, making provision for their journey back to Hereford. In his will a sum had been allocated to cover their expenses. Led by John de Clare, who had now taken over the running of the household, they took with them the three caskets, two containing the bones, the third with the heart.

In T. F. Tout's account of Thomas's life the bones were brought back by Richard Swinfield, who had been with Thomas in Italy. There is, however, no mention in any document of Swinfield being in Italy at that time. Though he had served in Thomas's household for eighteen years, from September 1281 to July 1282 he was Archdeacon of London. Pecham's register contains mandates, dated May and June 1282, addressed to him there.

It was late September when Pecham learned that Thomas was dead. At once he appointed Adam de Hales to act as his official at Hereford. He also informed the Dean and Chapter that he would be visiting them at the cathedral. The visitation – this would be no mere visit – would be done in style with a grand procession into the cathedral. They should expect him on 15th October.

The Dean and Chapter objected. Pecham would not be welcome. He had refused to allow the burial of Thomas's bones in Hereford Cathedral. He was even unwilling to allow them into England. Thomas, the Archbishop maintained, was excommunicate; his bones should not be buried in holy ground.[1]

According to Pecham's *Itinerarium*, he did arrive on the appointed day, processed in grand style through the cathedral then preached at length in the chapter house. The next day, the record states, he dealt with Robert of Gloucester, who had called to ask, with much humility, for the penalties against him to be revoked. This Pecham did – on condition that Robert paid one hundred pounds as surety for his obedience, made a pilgrimage to the Holy Land, presented twenty pounds of wax, or candles, to Canterbury at the same time placing a written promise of obedience on Becket's shrine ... the list went on. What's more there was a deadline of 25th November the same year. How much of all these labours Robert achieved, if any at all, is not clear, nor the truth of the *Itinerarium*. Certainly the Dean and Chapter refused to agree to the October visit and made their objections plain. Even so Pecham announced that he would be arriving on 5th December. Two days before, on 3rd December, he met the precentor of Hereford, William de Montfort, at Leominster. William handed him a letter with the red seal of a Roman penitentiary. It was dated 5th September 1282 and was from Galfridus de Sheppey stating that he had given Thomas absolution and penance and that this had been confirmed by Martin IV.

Pecham chose to ignore the letter, warning the Hereford canons that should they try to bury Thomas's bones in sacred ground they would be under penalty of interdict. He insisted that the excommunication issued by him at Lambeth still stood.

At some point on their journey home word of Pecham's attitude to Thomas's remains, what amounted to a kind of posthumous revenge, reached the household. Wisely, John de Clare took evading action. He stayed behind in the French port of Wissant with the two caskets containing the bones. There is no record of when he brought them to England. He must have done so quickly, secretly. It is said, in *Acta Sanctorum*, a record of the lives of saints, that, as he rode with the caskets through Canterbury, blood started to drip from them onto the ground. The bones were bleeding.

Where they were kept for the next few months is a mystery. Most likely John de Clare hid them somewhere, ensuring that they were guarded night and day. Then on 20th January 1283, a gathering of councillors and churchmen was held at Northampton. Edmund, Earl of Cornwall, first cousin of the King, who was one of the royal commissioners, broached the matter with Pecham. There was the question of the bones of Thomas Cantilupe; arrangements should be made for their burial. He was sure the Archbishop would agree that the matter had been too long delayed.

The Earl, who like his father Richard of Cornwall, was a man of tact and diplomacy, somehow managed to win Pecham round. John de Lewes, one of Pecham's notaries, recorded that the two caskets containing the bones were placed on the altar of Saint Andrew's, the

Northampton church. There, standing before them, Pecham gave his approval for their burial.

So at last they were taken to Hereford where, in the Lady Chapel at the east end of the cathedral, the caskets were placed under a large flat slab, the type used for senior churchmen and nobility.

And the heart? Thomas had bequeathed his heart to Edmund, Earl of Cornwall, who had founded a monastery of the Order of Bonhommes at Ashridge, near Berkhamstead. According to Holinshed, the Earl is said to have brought from Germany a box containing Christ's blood, two-thirds of which was kept, or possibly poured out, inside the monastery church at Ashridge. This story would have made a deep impression on Thomas and for his heart to be there in this 'house of the blood of Jesus Christ' as it is known in the Calendar of Wills, must have been his dearest wish. And though exactly when is unclear, according to *Acta Sanctorum*, the casket was eventually buried in the choir of the church.

Despite allowing the burial of Thomas's bones, Pecham could not forget his dislike of the man; perhaps it went too deep. And the appointment of Thomas's successor must have strengthened his old animosity. Richard Swinfield was a devoted friend and admirer of Thomas. His appointment, approved by the crown, showed clearly where Edward's sympathies lay.

In August 1284, the second anniversary of Thomas's death, Pecham granted an indulgence (a remission of temporal penalties) of twenty days in exchange for prayers for the soul of his late enemy. This was not an implication on Pecham's part that Thomas particularly needed prayers. Indulgences were frequently granted for prayers for the dead.

151

Soon after Thomas died the Bishop of Worcester, Geoffrey Giffard, had offered forty days indulgence to all those who would pray devoutly for Thomas at Hereford. The offer had been meant as a tribute to his late colleague and friend, a demonstration of support and sympathy, while showing Pecham how his own allegiance stood. The same was probably true of the Bishops of London and Rochester who made similar offers in subsequent years.

But Pecham may have had a less straightforward motive. To grant indulgences on behalf of the man known to have been his adversary, would make him appear as magnanimous, an example of Christian forgiveness. It may also have had something to do with the visit to Leominster he made that year to solve the problem over the Priory Church, succeeding where Thomas had failed. The indulgence for Thomas would round the matter off. It might even, by the grace of God, end his animosity. Perhaps he genuinely hoped it would.

Three years later, at the end of March 1287, an incident took place at Thomas's grave, a sick woman lying close by was suddenly cured.[2] Edith Oldecriste, the woman in question was the wife of Robert, the ironmonger of Hereford. For some time she had been behaving violently, possibly due to post-natal depression, possibly, as her husband insisted, due to alcoholism. Having clawed him with her nails, bitten her mother's nose, or finger, screamed at the neighbours, worse still, blasphemed against God, Robert had been forced to restrain the *furiosa* (a term for a mentally disturbed female) with woollen bindings, engaging two women to look after her. Eventually, on his neighbours' advice, he had measured her with a length of string and prepared two candles. (This long-established custom involved threading the measured string through a candle, which was then burnt as an offering at the shrine.) He had then loaded Edith, still tightly bound, into a large basket with one of the candles and carried her to the cathedral and then up into the rood loft to the Chapel of the Holy Cross, where he deposited her in front of the altar. After several days Edith, shrieking loudly, was bundled from the rood loft to Thomas's grave in the Lady Chapel. It was on Thursday 28th April, while Robert was taking the second candle to the Holy Cross at Winstanton, that the cure took place. Returning to Hereford, Robert heard the sound of the cathedral bells and a man ran to meet him with the news. He found that Edith had regained her sanity, she was completely calm.

A miracle. A genuine heaven-sent miracle. And though her recovery could be ascribed either to Thomas or to the Holy Rood, Edith had no doubt that the blessed Lord Thomas was responsible. She had seen him in a vision. What greater proof? It was certainly enough for Swinfield's almoner, Gilbert de Cheveninge, who had actually been there to witness Edith's recovery, part of it at least, at the Cantilupe shrine.

In celebration the bells were rung and a *Te Deum* sung exultantly.

The miracle was marvellous news, not only for Edith and her family, but for the cathedral and for Hereford. This was what Swinfield had been waiting for, and doubtless fervently praying for, a convincing miracle to start things off. Once the news spread others would come, the crippled, the diseased; there would be many hundreds thronging round the grave desperate to be cured. And it would happen, they

153

would be cured; the blessed Lord Thomas would see to it. That he was not yet officially canonized was of no concern. There were many holy men and women who were worshipped after death for their miraculous powers, those such as Alphege, Waltheof, Simon de Montfort … And Thomas would be canonized in time. Saint Thomas of Hereford. How right it sounded. The cathedral would be the focus of a cult, a place of pilgrimage so great that it would rival Canterbury. And, as at Canterbury, there would be offerings at the shrine; money, jewellery, silver, gold; the cathedral would grow rich.

This was Swinfield's dream. A year earlier he had written to two of the Hereford proctors in Italy asking them to find out whether any miracles had occurred by Thomas's grave at Saint Severo, also to discover the Pope's attitude towards Thomas's canonization.

Swinfield had no illusions about the time such proceedings were bound to take, always supposing they happened at all, a decision which depended on the Pope. But that had not prevented him from laying plans, nor from setting them in train. Indeed he was ready to launch the cult of Thomas Cantilupe.

Immediately the miracle had been recognized and the clamour of the bells had rung unexpectedly across the air, word of Edith's cure spread through the town. This was news worth hearing. It brought fresh hope to the hundreds who suffered from illness or disability, whom the *medici*, the monk-physicians, barber-surgeons, even, *in extremis*, the village wizards, had failed to cure.

The next morning Gilbert de Cheveninge was summoned by Canon Thomas St Omer, a long-serving member of the Hereford Chapter, who, Canon Capes implies, had sided against Thomas from the start of the Pecham dispute. As he was now Pecham's official for Llandaff, perhaps that is true. Canon St Omer castigated Gilbert for publicizing the news of this alleged miracle without the authority of the Archbishop. In any case, he told Gilbert, the miracle had been performed by Robert de Bethune, a Hereford bishop who had died in 1170 and was buried in the cathedral. St Omer suspended Gilbert for one week, a punishment greater than it sounds.

This was because on the following Thursday – it was Maundy Thursday when crowds would be flocking to Hereford for the Easter celebrations – a significant ceremony would take place; Thomas's bones would be transferred from the Lady Chapel to a new tomb in the recently completed north transept, where there was light and space.

To accusations that the relocation of the bones was unauthorized, Swinfield replied that it had been Thomas's wish to be buried in the north transept. He had begun to plan the new tomb soon after Thomas died and with it the rebuilding of that part of the cathedral. We know from the cathedral archives that in 1282–3 Pecham issued an indulgence to those who gave money towards the fabric of the building and that other bishops made similar offers between 1284 and 1291. It would be interesting to know what Pecham said, or thought privately, about the creation of this elaborate tomb for the interment of his adversary. Swinfield originally intended it as an altar tomb where pilgrims could kneel and pray. The upper section, the canopy, was added a few years later possibly as a sacred space to house a reliquary containing the bones, with its surrounding arches wide enough for pilgrims to push their heads through, to be closer to the sacred relics. The stone base is surrounded on three sides by beautifully carved figures of fourteen knights known as the 'weepers'. Perhaps they represent Cantilupe relations mourning the death of their kinsman. Or perhaps they are crusaders who stand for good overcoming the evil which is there, beneath their feet, the cowering creatures below each one. Above them the entwining foliage is very much of the Herefordshire school of carving, and, though long since removed, once, set into the top, was a brass of St Ethelbert, the cathedral's patron saint.[3]

In 1998 the tomb, or shrine, was cleaned and restored so that, catching the light through the lofty windows, the stone appears as pale as when it was new and, apart from the canopy, the whole memorial must look much as it did when it was completed in 1287.

It was on Maunday Thursday, 3rd April 1287, that Thomas's bones were transferred to the new shrine. It was a great occasion, a service of solemn magnificence, of the full ceremonial of the Church, and, in the presence of the great and the good, allegedly of the King himself. The day was a landmark for Hereford.

That Edward was there, if indeed he was, for records vary, was significant. Then, aged forty-nine, at the height of his powers, he was a figure of considerable authority, and the fact that he had come to Hereford, that he had taken time between returning from Gascony and preparing to go on crusade in June, showed how highly he regarded Thomas. He had valued him as a wise councillor, as a trusted friend, and for his goodness and piety. Which was surely why, in the years ahead, he wrote repeatedly to the papal court, as well as to seventeen cardinals, requesting that Thomas be canonized, and that in doing so he was motivated more by personal reasons than by national pride in acquiring a new English saint.

And Pecham, was he also there? As Archbishop he should have played a major part. For the sake of appearances, the good of his soul, perhaps he did.

It was immediate, the effect of the translation of the bones. Their miraculous powers were released; the air around the shrine was charged with the Lord Thomas's healing spirit. Within hours, it seems, few in Hereford had not heard of the *furiosa's* cure; and that same day, on Maunday Thursday, several others claimed they had been cured. By the following morning the news had spread beyond the city walls and from the village of Sugwas a woman brought her crippled daughter, Juliana, in a wicker basket and laid her beside Thomas's shrine. All at once, as she lay there, Juliana noticed the man on the stretcher close to her was standing up, he was walking round the shrine. Gilbert, the minstrel, crippled for years; was suddenly cured. And then to her amazement she found she was able to raise herself, she could step out of her basket. She could walk. Her heart must have danced, if not her legs.

The power of suggestion? Or, as she claimed, a miracle wrought by the blessed Lord Thomas who, appearing in a vision, had ordered her to stand and use her legs. Her word was quite good enough for the tomb custodians, one of whom was Gilbert de Cheveninge returned after his week's expulsion, who happily recorded another cure. Once again the cathedral bells rang out and a *Te Deum* was sung, though as it was Good Friday perhaps this was delayed till Saturday.

And with the ringing of the bells came yet another

cure; a woman named Matilda, who suffered from dementia, claimed sudden, miraculous recovery. The following day, Easter Sunday, she met Julia, who was scornful of her cure. Matilda's sickness healed by the Lord Thomas? Julia very much doubted it. Yet as she spoke she went blind in one eye. A punishment for her disbelief. Matilda hurried her to the shrine where, overcome with remorse, she confessed her sin. And her sight returned.

It was at the beginning, in those first few weeks, that the rate of miracles was at its height. Of the roughly five hundred cures recorded between 1287 and 1312, seventy-one took place during April alone. The majority of the early pilgrims came from Hereford or close by. But soon there were those from further off, suppliants from outlying villages who had endured being trundled along rough country lanes in barrows or carts to reach the source of the miraculous power. For the news had travelled far, joyful and sensational news, doubtless growing in the telling. Yet the proof was there in those who had been cured. The winter had passed, there was hope in the air. It was Eastertide.

One pilgrim who arrived on Holy Saturday was Milo Pychard, a distinguished knight of the shire, *famosus et notus*, as the record puts it – he was later to become sheriff of Herefordshire. His status explains why Bishop Swinfield had personally invited him to the Easter ceremonies. There was another more cogent reason. Six years earlier Milo Pychard had been seriously injured in a tournament and had suffered ever since. As soon as he heard of the miraculous cures taking place at Thomas's shrine, he set off from Strangford, near Ross on Wye, not a great distance but for Milo a slow and painful one.

158

On Easter Sunday, Milo Pychard, kneeling at the shrine, found his pain had gone; he rose from his knees. He was completely cured.

This particular miracle, widely acclaimed, was effective in attracting others of Milo's class, the landowners and nobility, to visit the shrine. Generally, however, records show the majority of pilgrims came from lower down the social scale. This may in part be explained by the reluctance of the nobility to acknowledge ill health. Any kind of infirmity, even a disease such as leprosy, was regarded as a sign of weakness, of imperfection, a matter of shame. The wealthy were also more likely to call in a physician, being able to pay for his services. On the other hand amongst the poorer people, those for whom life was a continuing struggle to keep dry and warm, to get hold of food – there was seldom enough – disease of all kinds was commonplace. A contributory factor was the primitive sewage, which, particularly in towns, contaminated the water supply. Medical treatment, if it could be afforded, would be blood-letting or amputation, followed by gangrene as often as not, followed by death. No wonder the poor were eager for a miracle.

In a recent study the consultant, John Ross, analysed a number of the cures attributed to Thomas. With the help of the late archivist of Hereford Cathedral, Meryl Jancey, he researched the Vatican records of testimonies given at the canonization hearings, then, choosing half a dozen cases and having examined them individually, he gave a medical diagnosis with a possible explanation of each one. The results, published in the *British Medical Journal* in December 1987, show the miracles from a modern medical viewpoint. They also show the power of suggestion, of mind over matter, and of faith in Thomas's healing power.

One case involved Alice de Lonsdale, who herself testified before the commissioners in 1307. Fourteen years earlier, as a small girl she had been on her way to the shrine of Saint James at Compostella with her father, William, when she had tripped over a hole in the road and broken the bones in her right foot. That night, struck by fever, she had lost the use of her left limbs and her right leg. For the next ten years she and her father had lived on the streets of London, begging for alms while her right foot had become increasingly swollen with putrefaction. By chance William had heard of Thomas Cantilupe and, vowing to dedicate Alice to Saint Mary if she was cured, he pushed her in a 'one-wheeled cart' all the way to Hereford. After three days and nights praying at the shrine Alice had a vision in which a beautiful old man in white clothes, silvery as a lily, anointed her body with a milky substance from a little box, touching her from her breasts downwards. Following her vision her wounds dried up; within a week she had been able to walk with a stick.

John Ross suggests a number of possible causes for Alice de Lonsdale's paralysis, the most likely being a 'paradoxical' embolus from a venous thrombosis in the right leg associated with the infection. He adds that her recovery was remarkable.

A more simple diagnosis was possible in the case of John from Hamme, (now known as Holme Lacy) who had a tumour the size of his fist on the back of his neck. In praying to Thomas, he had put his head and shoulders through an opening in the side of the tomb to be closer to the sacred bones. When he withdrew his head, the tumour had gone. John Ross concludes that the tumour was a large sebaceous cyst which had ruptured as John from Hamme forced his head through the opening. Whether the aperture was one of the arches surrounding the present canopy, which measure 29cm × 32cm, or part of an earlier structure, is not clear.

Another case concerned Thomas's servant, Hugh le Barber, an important witness at the hearings in 1307. It was one evening not long after Thomas died, when Hugh, who must have been in his late forties, was dining out in London with his wife. Suddenly he felt a sharp pain in his head, his right eye seemed full of ashes so that he could not see. The next morning the pain struck his left eye too; he found he was blind. The application of a plaster by a surgeon brought him out in a distressing rash. The blindness remained and though he prayed daily to Thomas and the Blessed Mary, it was not until he was measured to Thomas (with a string, to be inserted into a candle) and wax models of his eyes were sent to Thomas's birthplace at Hamleden, that gradually his sight returned. After two days Hugh could see hens walking about outside his house. A year later his vision was clear enough to play chess and dice. John Ross concludes Hugh's sudden blindness with slow but almost complete recovery was probably caused by iritis with spontaneous remission but, with so little to go by, the cause is impossible to define.

Hugh's recovery was an example of a miracle happening remote from the shrine, several of which are noted in the Vatican records. One concerned Richard d'Insula who was afflicted with verrucas all over his hands and feet. While in Orleans he happened to hear of Thomas and at once began to pray to him. Twenty-four hours later the verrucas began to disappear; after three days only one remained.

Other long distance miracles involved inanimate objects. A ship on its way from Gascony with a cargo of wine was caught in a storm in the Irish Sea. The master commanded his crew to pray to Thomas; the storm died away. Another alleged miracle involved a house which the owner claimed to have seen in a vision engulfed in flames. Hurriedly praying and bending a penny to Thomas, the flames died down; his house was saved.

The rite of bending a penny, like that of measuring, was believed to effect a miracle. In an unusual case a penny was bent over a falcon, belonging to a Cornish knight; the falcon, badly damaged, had been trampled by a horse. Gently cradled in the knight's hood, the bird revived. And a measuring to Thomas brought Felicia's mare, apparently lying dead in a field, back to life.

Such a measuring, the length of a full size mare, would have produced a wick for a very long candle to be burnt at the shrine. As candles, sometimes as much as four feet high, were often used in churches, this was quite acceptable, but when it came to measuring land boundaries, five hundred arm-lengths, for instance, or the perimeter of a house, even with the wick folded several times, the resulting candle was a massive size. At the peak of the cult with a positive forest of candles planted round the shrine, the north transept must have blazed with their flickering light, the smell of molten wax and considerable heat adding to the febrile atmosphere. Even in 1291 when the cult was declining and far fewer pilgrims visited the tomb, the value of the candle wax burned throughout the year was, according to *Taxatio*

Nicholai, about twenty pounds, roughly ten thousand pounds today. According to custom the value of surplus wax, above that needed for lighting, belonged to the cathedral treasurer. When, in 1289, the Dean and Chapter decided to claim a share, it was agreed that Luke, the treasurer, was entitled to two-thirds and the Chapter the rest. When soon afterwards Luke died, the arrangement was renegotiated, presumably in favour of the new treasurer. For he was John de Swinfield, a kinsman of the bishop.

It was not only the heat and the almost psychedelic effect of the candle light that made the north transept more like bedlam than any kind of holy place. Pilgrims thronged around the tomb, struggling to get close, pushing between stretchers, barrows, baskets. There was constant noise, wailing, groaning, the murmuring of prayers, the crying of children, staccato shrieks. The atmosphere of such intense emotion often brought on hysterics with screaming, writhing and falling to the floor, which was filthy with excrement, vomit, blood. Lurking among these sufferers were those with a rather different aim, thieves of all kinds; the cutpurse who would deftly slice the purse from a traveller's belt, or the 'pilgrim' in disguise, who, hobbling to the tomb, would kneel and reverently kiss the stone while he snatched up coins left as offerings. A skilled thief would scoop up money with his tongue and carry it away concealed in his mouth.

On guard for such crooks were the custodians, *custodes*, who would make frequent collections of coins and, possibly, jewellery. But not everything of value was rounded up; an inventory of offerings made by the canonization commissioners in 1307 included five silver ships, precious stones, gold rings, as well as anchors, knives and some two thousand wax images of body parts; there were also a number of human limbs. The *custodes* kept a record of miraculous cures. A medieval drawing shows a *custos* seated at a lectern beside a tomb ready to note down another cure. Of course cures had to be genuine though most custodians were probably happy to take the recipient's word for it; the more effective Thomas's powers proved to be the more popular the shrine. Pilgrims brought offerings, funds for the upkeep of the cathedral and for Swinfield's extensive building plans.

They also brought income to the city, for pilgrims were medieval tourists; some had travelled far to Hereford, they spent money at taverns on bed and board, they boosted local trade. The more gullible, and those with coins to spare, bought relics, small objects said to have belonged to Thomas, scraps of cloth from his cloak, a hair from his beard, a small piece of bone. Almost all were completely bogus, worthless other than as souvenirs.

By no means every pilgrim came to be cured. Many sought forgiveness, a lessening of their time in purgatory, by praying at the shrine, also by earning indulgences. These were offered by clergy to those who visited the shrine of a saint and were granted, in return for prayers, pilgrimages, charitable deeds or, as was most welcome in this instance, by contributing to the cost of a sacred building. In 1289 the Bishop of Salisbury offered twenty days for a visit to Thomas's shrine and made a contribution to the cathedral fabric fund. Most offers of indulgence were quite flexible so that those who were too busy, or too lazy, for the journey could make an offering instead. From those who did make a visit, an offering at the shrine was also expected. For the cathedral the arrangement was most satisfactory; either way they stood to benefit.

But, though year after year a succession of bishops offered further indulgences, the response was increasingly disappointing, as time went by pilgrim numbers fell, correspondingly so did the offerings.

Looking back it seems that the popularity of Thomas's cult began to decline almost as soon as it began. After the sensational Eastertide following the translation of the bones – there were five cures alone on 3rd April, the opening day – the figures for May were roughly half, thirty-eight against seventy-one; in June there were eighteen miracles, in July eleven, by December the number was down to two. Altogether for the year, from April 1287 to April 1288, the tally was about one hundred and sixty miracles. In contrast for the whole of the thirteenth century, from 1287 to the end of 1299, the total was roughly two hundred and fifty.

Yet perhaps dry figures make the fall-off sound worse than it was for, through time, the pattern changed. Records show that as enthusiasm among local people waned, more long distance pilgrims visited the shrine. Word of Thomas's powers would have spread by chance; a wandering minstrel, a pedlar perhaps, talking to a stranger might mention the goings-on at Hereford; '… at the tomb of the Lord Thomas … a miracle … 'tis true, they say … one blind from birth and all of a sudden … and a child drowned, brought back from the dead …' Such stories guaranteed an audience for, in the Middle Ages, religion was very much part of life, not always benign but forever there, as was illness; both affected everyone, rich and poor, both were newsworthy.

Of the pilgrims who came from 'foreign' parts the majority were men. This was partly because, owing to the hazards of travel, women tended to avoid long journeys. Wives of noblemen, with the women of the household, would move together to another castle or manor, but lower down the social scale women, most of them child-bound, would remain at home.

This preponderance of male pilgrims visiting the shrine altered the balance of the first few months when there were far more women suppliants. The figures for April 1287 of recognized cures were forty-five women to twenty-five men.

It may be that women are generally more trusting, more gullible perhaps. In 1287 Edith's recovery had given them hope; they believed Thomas would cure them too. And without delay they would hurry to the shrine. Men, on the other hand, preferred to wait for proof of Thomas's powers.

Another variation in the pattern was the gradual increase in cures occurring away from the shrine. It was believed that Thomas's sanctity grew in strength so that its healing effect could connect with those at a distance from the tomb. As a rule recovery was followed by a visit to give thanks and an offering, though, in some cases, distance may have ruled it out. In his book, *Miracles and Pilgrims*, the historian, Ronald Finucane, maps the location of miracles attributed to Thomas. Obviously most occurred round Hereford, but as the news spread outwards, cures were registered at places as far away as Suffolk, North Wales, Devon, even Ireland.

How powerful an aura came from Thomas's knife, a piece of his hair shirt or iron-link belt is hard to imagine. But these with other smaller relics, shreds of clothing, tiny fragments of bone, were the centre of subsidiary shrines at Leominster, Winchester, Hambleden, his birthplace, and, most importantly, at Ashridge where his heart had been interred.

In 1290 Richard Swinfield appealed to Pope Nicholas IV to consider the canonization of Thomas. Swinfield was aware that, before he became pope in 1288, Nicholas IV had been Cardinal Jerome of Oporto, who had celebrated Thomas's Requiem Mass at San Severo, and delivered the eulogy, a sermon in Thomas's praise. He must have reckoned, therefore, that Pope Nicholas would regard the canonization favourably and possibly encourage it.

Shrewdly, Swinfield must have made sure his papal appeal was widely known for records show that it coincided with a marked widening of the pilgrimage geography, the catchment area, to use a modern phrase. In the next few years a number of other bishops also appealed, and made their action known, which may account for the slight rise in numbers visiting the shrine after 1290. The accounts kept by the cathedral chaplain, John de Brecone, show that for the year from Michaelmas 1290 to 1291, offerings at the tomb totalled £178 10s 7d, (equal to about one hundred thousand pounds today). This went a long way to meeting the bills for Swinfield's rebuilding programme, which, with repairs added in, came to £286 1s 8½d. As the average offering was probably a penny, this gives some idea of the numbers of pilgrims involved, even then, when, compared with 1287, the crowds were small.

Building work at that time is thought to have been mainly on the inner north porch and the nave aisle, the aim being to give better access to the shrine in the north transept. At a later stage, though exactly when is not clear, the work progressed to the north choir aisle and the north east transept. It has been suggested that Swinfield designed this as a ceremonial route to the Lady Chapel, where eventually he intended to create a far more splendid shrine. It seems likely that his overall plan included lining the north choir aisle with the tombs of former bishops, among them his own and those of his relations. Unlike the simple Norman architecture of the nave, choir and south transept, this late thirteenth-century rebuilding of the north side of the cathedral was in the graceful Early English style with its pointed arches and delicate carving. Hugh le Barber, testifying before the commissioners in 1307, told of how the work had included a beautiful bell tower decorated with ball-flowers. According to Hugh, the bell tower as well as all the other building had been funded entirely from legacies and offerings at Thomas's shrine.

This, it seems, was not quite the case – a slight rose-tinting of Hugh's memory perhaps – though the commission did record that the offerings had been enough for part of the great tower as well as two new naves, *duabus navibus ampliata*. Whether the word *navis* refers to an aisle or a bay is not clear.

The bell tower, with its elaborate carving, was undoubtedly beautiful; it was also of great height and massive weight. The weight was too much for the old foundations; they began to show signs of giving way. And by then, notwithstanding Hugh's claim, funds were running out. Now in the early fourteenth century, few pilgrims came.

Then in 1319, Swinfield's successor, Adam de Orleton, appealed to Pope John XXII. Would the Holy Father allow him to appropriate the revenue from the church at Shinfield in Berkshire (one of the cathedral's richest benefices), with its nearby chapel at Swallowfield, towards the fabric fund? Bishop Orleton went into great detail, explaining that skilled builders had judged the old foundations sound, that enormous sums had already been spent, more than twenty thousand marks, in fact, but that recent signs of weakness in the foundations meant that the only solution was completely to rebuild, an exceedingly expensive operation. Recent building repairs, as well as expenses incurred by the canonization enquiry, had drained their funds. The financial situation was desperate ...

It may be there was a touch of exaggeration in Bishop Orleton's portrayal of the state of the foundations for there is no record of a major rebuilding following his appeal. Nonetheless it was effective. A few months later came a papal bull allowing the Chapter to use the rents from Shinfield and Swallowfield for the fabric fund 'so long as the work shall last'. (This arrangement still stands.)

When Richard Swinfield died in 1217 Thomas had not yet been canonized nor had the new shrine been built. Swinfield left one hundred marks towards it in his will; he also left money towards the building of a new chapter house, though that did not happen till 1364. He was buried in the north choir aisle, as he must have wished, with other members of his family nearby. His tomb is quite plain, his inscription simply his name and dates. If there was once an effigy on top, it must have been stolen or destroyed. When the tomb was opened in 1861 there was nothing inside other than the body encased in lead and an episcopal ring.

Did Swinfield die with a sense of frustration and deep disappointment? The aim he had worked so hard to bring about, Thomas's canonization, had not been achieved. Nor had the Lady Chapel shrine been built. Perhaps his spirit haunted the north choir aisle till both these missions had been fulfilled.

Chapter XII

During the first millennium when the rules of the Church were made locally, canonization was a simple decision taken by the bishop of the diocese to which the person in question had belonged. The bishop, or sometimes the provincial synod, would consider the life of one of the 'faithful departed' known for their charity, their holiness, their miraculous powers or martyrdom, and judge accordingly. There was no formal enquiry; the Pope was not involved. Even when Rome did begin to intervene – the earliest known papal canonization was in 993 – the procedure was comparatively simple, a survey of the candidate's life and works, their *acta*. But, as year by year papal canonization increased, more and more laws were introduced until by the end of the thirteenth century the process had grown into a legal maze of officialdom, which inevitably took many years to complete, three decades in Thomas's case.

Richard Swinfield, who had been determined on Thomas's canonization since his death, first wrote to the Pope putting forward his predecessor's case in

April 1290. Swinfield was not the only one to write. In 1305, when a committee of enquiry was eventually appointed, it transpired that, at various times, letters had also been received from Edward I, the Archbishop of York, fifteen bishops, seven abbots, eleven counts, as well as numerous barons and noblemen, all proclaiming Thomas's virtues and miraculous powers. The seventeen of these letters that have survived are remarkably similar. The historian, Patrick Daly, suggests that Swinfield circulated a blueprint to his fellow bishops to ensure they petitioned effectively. Edward too, preoccupied with various crises at the time, had, at his own request, been helped with the wording of his letter by two canons who had ridden to London specially to do so.[1]

It was the newly-elected Pope Clement V, who issued a mandate for the preliminary enquiry to begin. At the time he was touring in his native Gascony with a skeleton staff and a minimum of official documents, certainly no notes on Thomas Cantilupe. But he wrote to the papal Curia instructing three cardinals to look into the circumstances of Thomas's life and miracles. While this was going on, the Hereford Chapter, unaware of Clement's mandate, set up their own commission to look into local miracles.

Once Clement received the result of the three cardinals' preliminary search, which was favourable, he appointed three commissioners to examine the evidence in detail so that a judgement could be made. The commissioners were William Testa, Ralph Baldock and William Durand. Testa, the papal nuncio, was one of the officers recently entrusted with the administration of the province and diocese of Canterbury. This had been necessitated by the absence of Archbishop Winchelsey, who, following a dispute with Edward, had left the country, and meant that Testa had little time for the enquiry. Ralph Baldock, Bishop of London, was appointed Chancellor of England a week after the enquiry opened. As Edward had died near Carlisle two weeks before that – he had been ill for some time but had refused to give up and had been carried on a litter to Scotland to deal with the latest rebellion – Bishop Baldock probably had even less time than Testa to give to the enquiry. This meant that Durand, who was the Bishop of the southern French diocese of Mende, was left with the main burden of the work. However, as he was highly competent and an expert in canon law, he was well able to manage this.

Though Durand arrived in England in February 1307, the start of the enquiry was delayed when somebody raised the question of Pecham's excommunication of Thomas. Had it been valid? Did it still stand? Clement at once instructed the commissioners to look into the matter, a certain barrier to sainthood if it proved true. But after two months of investigation during which forty-four witnesses were questioned and sheafs of documents examined, they came to the conclusion that Thomas had died reconciled to the Church. The enquiry could begin.[2]

Which it did in the chapter house of St Paul's Cathedral on 13th July. The three commissioners sat on one side with three or four notaries who wrote furiously and continuously, the staccato scratching of their quills an unrelenting background accompaniment. Facing them was the postulator, Canon Henry de Schorne, the proctor representing the petitioning party, who was there to press his case to promote Thomas as a candidate for sainthood. As a Doctor of

Canon Law and a devoted supporter of Thomas, Henry de Schorne was well qualified and extremely keen. He had been one of the canons who had helped Edward to draft his letter to the Pope. Moreover, in April 1306, he had travelled all the way to the Curia to nudge the case along.

The enquiry followed a pre-arranged order with questions listed under rubrics or general headings, so that each witness, having taken his place in the middle of the room and sworn to tell the truth, gave his evidence accordingly. The first set of questions, of a fairly general nature, concerned Thomas's life, his youth, his life-style, faith, reputation; these were followed by more detailed and specific questions, known as the *interrogatoria*, which concentrated mainly on the miracles. Both sides were able to call witnesses, and while those summoned by Henry de Schorne were full of praise for Thomas, there were a number called by the commissioners, most of them Franciscans from monasteries round London or Hereford, who denied any knowledge of the miracles and who did so in distinctly dismissive tones. Most likely this reflected Thomas's dispute with the Franciscan Pecham.

The commissioners had not summoned these witnesses in an adversarial sense. Unlike Schorne their position was impartial; they were there to collect sworn testimony from as wide a range of witnesses as possible. In fact they called only twenty-nine; Schorne called one hundred and fifty-two. In the cases of witnesses too ill to attend, the notaries went to their homes to take evidence. Another problem for the notaries was the translation of spoken evidence into ecclesiastical Latin. Many churchmen gave their evidence in Latin or Norman

French, the language of the aristocracy, while most lay people used everyday English. A handful from the Marches testified in Welsh.

The longest evidence given at St Paul's came from the sixth witness, Hugh le Barber. By then, twenty-five years after Thomas's death, Hugh was over seventy, his memory was patchy and sometimes confused, particularly of the early years. He had first known Thomas when he was employed as his barber at Paris University, well over half a century before.

His testimony, translated and set out by the late archivist of Hereford Cathedral, Meryl Jancey, is simple and often rather touching, revealing almost as much about humble, uncomplicated, selfless Hugh, as it does about his master. But because of his extreme devotion to Thomas his testimony is distinctly biased. Thomas, in Hugh's eyes, was completely faultless. He was faithful, truthful, abstemious in eating and drinking, also in speaking; he lived an austere and disciplined life yet, being no hypocrite and not wanting to appear better than his fellows, he conformed in outward appearance and kept such self-inflicted penances as his hair belt carefully concealed. Hugh made clear that the Lord Thomas was diligent in caring for his many parishioners and in keeping them in order, though he never entered into litigation unless he was sure he was in the right. Others might have added that, having undertaken legal action, no one pursued it more relentlessly. But not Hugh. Nor the many others who had worked with Thomas and known him well and who, looking back, saw his virtues as even greater than in life. Besides, they wanted him to be canonized. The commissioners were surely aware of that and of the tendency to enhance his image.

It is possible that Durand referred to this when, at the end of the enquiry, he wrote to Pope Clement with a long report on the whole procedure. Possible, but unlikely, for it was not up to the commissioners to influence the judgement in any way. Judgement was the business of the Curia, which could not begin until they had received the evidence.

The hearings lasted for four months. After four weeks in London, from 13th July to 12th August, Durand and Baldock – Testa was apparently occupied elsewhere – rode to Hereford. On 29th August they inspected the tomb and the offerings placed round it before the second stage of interviews began. On the closing day, 12th November, so many witnesses were still waiting to report on miracles that the commissioners, pressed by Schorne and other Hereford officials, allowed a list of their statements to be included in the report. Then sifted, corrected and set in order, the mass of evidence was taken to the Curia.

Once it arrived, which allowing for winter weather, was probably early in 1308, the Pope passed the report to a group of his chaplains, who examined it and arranged it under rubrics or general headings. Next it was the turn of the 'examiners'. These were three cardinals chosen by the Pope, one from each order or rank, a Cardinal Bishop, a Cardinal Priest and a Cardinal Deacon, whose task was to study the report and, for the first time, to evaluate it. Cardinals at that time had many responsibilities; they carried what we would call a heavy work load. Being human – some may have seen themselves as rather more – they tended to procrastinate, to shelve less urgent matters. In the case of Thomas they had some excuse, for in June 1308 further documents were added, one concerning the excommunication together with no less than six volumes on the original enquiry. Even allowing for this extra work there was no sign of progress after months, then years. Several times there were delays, the process was suspended, why was not disclosed. At each delay letters were dispatched from Hereford and from Edward II urging the Pope and various cardinals to move the case along. Edward also wrote to the King of France who had apparently shown interest in Thomas at the Council of Vienne in 1311 and who, with the papacy then based at Avignon, was able to exert some influence. Sure enough Thomas's file was unearthed, some work was done on it, lists were made. Then it was stowed away again. More letters were dispatched, also delegations, personal envoys from the King. They had little effect. It did not help that for two years there was no pope at all.

Then in 1316 John XXII, a Frenchman with a legal training who had been Cardinal Bishop of Porto, was elected pope. Hopeful of action, Edward launched a fresh batch of letters, but Pope John, involved in a dispute with the Franciscans, had other matters on his mind. It was not until the following year, when Adam de Orleton became Bishop of Hereford, that at last there were stirrings at the Curia. Bishop Orleton had been King's proctor at the papal court since 1305; he knew its workings – and its obstructions. It seems he also had influence, for it was probably the following summer that the cardinals at last presented their report. The next step was for the Pope and cardinals to meet in consistory council and make the decision on canonization. This took place, after further delay, in March 1320. It was the end of Lent. A decision was postponed until after Easter. Finally after much discussion Pope John XXII bowed in agreement.

Thomas Cantilupe was to be canonized. His feast day would be 2nd October.

On the morning of 17th April 1320, a great procession entered the church of Notre Dame des Doms in Avignon. At the heart of this great stream of cardinals, churchmen, civic dignitaries, all richly robed in full regalia, was Pope John XXII. Flanked by two senior cardinals he made his way to the pontifical throne and, after each cardinal had paid him homage, he preached on the text: 'He was tried and found perfect, and he shall be in glory.'

And then came the climax, the high-point of the canonization rite, the moment when the Pope made the mighty proclamation of Thomas's heroic sanctity. Finally, with much solemn chanting, the swinging of censers and frequent genuflection, the Mass was celebrated in honour of the newly-canonized saint, Thomas Cantilupe of Hereford.

Once the news reached England that, at last, it had happened, that the canonization had taken place, Bishop Orleton wrote to each parish in his diocese inviting everyone to come to the first celebration of the feast day of Saint Thomas in Hereford Cathedral on 2nd October. (The date matched his own installation as bishop.) Most likely the service was followed by further celebration; feasting, merriment, dancing in the streets. A brand new saint, their own Saint Thomas, was indeed something to celebrate.

What was lacking now was the shrine in the Lady Chapel, the much larger and more elaborate shrine than the one in the north transept, that had been planned long ago by Richard Swinfield and for which he had left money in his will. On 18th November the Archbishop of Canterbury, Walter Reynolds, wrote to all the clergy of the diocese urging them to give towards the building of the shrine. Two days later Edward II issued an appeal to the whole of England and Wales; he authorized seven Hereford proctors to tour the country collecting donations, he also instructed his own bailiffs to co-operate with the proctors. Edward's appeal was a great success. Everywhere large sums were raised; £45 4s 2d, for example, in one Norfolk archdeaconry alone, which today would be worth roughly twenty-seven thousand pounds.

At last work on the new shrine could go ahead, and from the cathedral accounts of that time it is clear that this was an exceptional design, a great elaborate edifice grand enough to glorify any saint. Perhaps Thomas would have thought it a touch too grand. The finest craftsmen in the country were employed; Michael, the image-maker of London, Adam the marbler, who had previously paved Saint Paul's, William Sprot of London, an expert in electrum, a kind of brass known as lattern used for monuments, whose account was £80, and the goldsmith, John de Werlingworthe, also of London, who made sundry ornaments for the shrine. The sixteenth-century antiquarian, John Leland, writes of Saint Thomas being 'rychely shrined', which so he must have been, eventually. But it was many years before that came about.

There were problems and delays, funds dwindled and then in 1327 came the death of Edward II. It was a grim death, almost certainly murder, giving him a kind of martyr status, which resulted in many pilgrims switching their devotions, and their offerings, to Gloucester, where he had been buried in the presbytery of the Abbey Church.[3] Nine years later so few candles were burnt at Thomas's shrine that Pope Benedict XII, realizing the dire financial situation, issued a mandate to reduce the tax levied on wax. On such a small amount it can have made little difference.

When in 1348 the Black Death swept through the land, all the cathedral building work came to a halt for about a year. Possibly this widespread plague triggered a rise in pilgrim numbers, though a rise so slight it had scant effect on the offerings.

Eventually, in the autumn of 1349, while the Black Death still poisoned the air, the great shrine in the Lady Chapel was ready for the translation of the bones. On Sunday 25th October, in the presence of Edward III, who had fallen ill on the journey but suddenly recovered – a miracle, undoubtedly – and a great throng of the great and the good, the tomb in the north transept was ceremoniously opened. Inside was a chest made of wood so fragile that it crumbled as the lid was raised. With careful fingers the bones and skull were lifted out and passed to the most privileged round the tomb to be held for a moment and reverently kissed. Then in solemn and stately procession the bones were carried to the Lady Chapel and placed in their magnificent new resting place. And there, according to the prayer read over them, they would remain until Resurrection Day.

At that point, quite suddenly, it was said, the plague died down, soon it was gone, remarkably, mysteriously. But surely there was no mystery. The blessed Thomas had intervened. Praise be Saint Thomas Cantilupe.

The bones did not remain till Resurrection Day. Two centuries later came the Reformation of the Roman Catholic church, the movement that led to the establishment of Protestanism and which, in England, was triggered by Henry's disagreement with the Vatican over his intention to divorce his first

180

wife, Catherine of Aragon. Having broken with Rome in 1529, after the failure of his Lord Chancellor, Cardinal Wolsey, to negotiate with the Pope, Henry ordered his new vicar-general, Thomas Cromwell, to oversee the destruction of all sacred shrines. Following that thorough and ruthless operation, Cromwell, full of zeal, set about the dissolution of the monasteries, a reform – or disaster for those loyal to Rome – bound to bring immense financial gain to the monarchy, for many abbeys and monasteries owned great wealth as well as property and land. For four years from 1536 to 1540, while first the smaller monasteries then the larger ones were ruthlessly closed down by Cromwell's forces, the King increasingly found fault with his vicar-general, till eventually, in 1540, Cromwell was accused of high treason and of 'being a detestable heretic' and executed.

Before Cromwell's wreckers reached their city many Herefordian Catholics realized the inevitable fate of the Cantilupe shrine in the Lady Chapel of the cathedral. How could a monument of such magnificence possibly escape demolition? And, as they feared, the enormous shrine was completely destroyed, but by then they had acted to remove its contents, the bones of their own venerable saint, who was still greatly loved.

Judging from small relics, including pieces of bone, later found in possession of the Cantilupe family, a certain amount must have been removed from the body even before it was interred in the first tomb. But most of the bones had remained together and when, probably about 1538, in what must have been a tense and clandestine operation, the shrine was opened, there they were, safe inside their casket.

An account of what happened to them following

their rescue was told by Fr John Morris, a Jesuit priest, in an article in *The Month* for January 1882. Fr Morris, who had been researching the history of the bones, discovered a document at Stonyhurst, in Elizabethan handwriting, listing their custodians after their removal from the shrine. The first was the Reverend William Ely, a Herefordian, ordained during Queen Mary's reign. For some years he was the President of St John's College, Cambridge, then returning to Hereford during Elizabeth I's reign he was imprisoned, presumably for his Catholic sympathies. He died in prison in 1609. Though his successor, the Reverend Cuffaud, gave away two of the bones, the rest remained in and around Hereford. It is believed that each bone was housed separately with a trustworthy Catholic family, that each was carefully guarded and its whereabouts kept secret – up to a point. Faithful Catholics knew where all of them were hidden and sometimes, probably for some particular reason, small groups would gather to venerate one or several of them.

On one occasion, though when is not clear, the bones were carried through the streets of Hereford at night in the hope that Saint Thomas would spare the city from a virulent plague that was spreading through the neighbouring villages.

During the Civil War, when Hereford remained staunchly Royalist, the bones were moved away from the city to save them from seizure by Cromwellian troops. Again this must have been done with great secrecy, each bone handled separately and carefully concealed. Perhaps one would be buried in a haybale, tucked inside a bundle or a saddlebag, then carried after dark to a destination few would know about. It is thought that they were constantly passed from place to place; certainly many seemed to disappear.

Though fortunately not quite all. After much devoted sleuthing by various prelates and historians the whereabouts of a few of these sacred relics has been traced.

Some thirty years after they were taken from the shrine, Brother Peter Street, a lay member of the Benedictine house of Lambstring in the diocese of Hildesheim in Germany, was visiting his sister in Hereford. There, in her house, Brother Peter found a skull which he identified, perhaps by its dark colour, perhaps by the exceptionally high and broad fore-head, as Thomas Cantilupe's. According to the Downside archive, Brother Peter 'not thinking it kept and exposed with dew public veneration, brought the same to Lambspring ...' There, each year on Saint Thomas's feast day, 2nd October, the Bishop of Hildesheim allowed the public veneration of this sacred relic.[4] And there it remained, despite requests from a number of Hereford clergy for its return. At last in September 1881 a monk of Downside, Dom Gilbert Dolan, travelled to Lambspring determined to find the missing skull. With the parish priest and the lay sacristan, who knew the building inside out, they thoroughly combed through the church, searching round each altar, through chests, cupboards. Nothing came to light. Then as Dom Gilbert was about to give up, the parish priest suggested one last possibility, a cupboard behind the High Altar. The cupboard appeared empty. The priest climbed on a chair and searched the upper shelf. That was empty too. He heaved the chair onto a table in order to reach an even higher shelf. And on it, pushed to the back, dusty and broken, were two boxes. He lifted them down, prized them open and there, inside one of them, lying on top of a jumble of relics, was an ancient skull. Leaning over the box the three men must have peered at it in the shadowy light. Could it be …? And almost at once their doubts dissolved for, through the netted cobwebs, they noted its colour was dark, reddish-brown; more significant still they could see that a section was missing from the forehead, an unusually high and intelligent forehead with considerable width between the eyes.

This, beyond all doubt, was the skull of Saint Thomas Cantilupe.

Dom Gilbert's certainty, and most likely that of his helpers, came from their knowledge of the account of the skull written in 1720 by Dom Benet Gibbon, a monk of Lambspring, describing how a piece of the forehead had been sawn out so that should the relic ever be removed from Lambspring, it could, when traced, be identified.

Whether Dom Gilbert took the skull back with him to Downside there and then is not clear. But that is where it is now in safekeeping – apart from one small piece. In 1959, in recognition of their centenary the monks of Belmont Abbey in Hereford received a present from Downside, a section of the precious skull, which may well be the piece originally cut out at Lambspring. At Belmont it is kept above one of the altars in a specially designed reliquary which each year on Thomas's feast day, 2nd October, is moved to the Sanctuary, where, on a table near the altar, it is placed between two candles, to be venerated at Mass and Vespers.

The history of another relic, one of Thomas's arm bones, was also recounted by Fr Morris. In 1651, Fr Cuffaud, the custodian of the relics at that time, gave this particular bone to another Catholic priest, Fr

John Poyntz, who passed it on to his sister, perhaps for safety's sake, for Mary Poyntz lived in Paris. Following her brother's instructions, Mary Poyntz gave the arm bone to the Jesuit College at Saint Omer, where it was placed in the chapel and allowed by the local bishop to be publicly venerated. When the college moved to Bruges the bone went too and after the college was closed down, the Bishop of Bruges took charge of it. And then? Who knows. But it is possible that somewhere in Belgium, inside a reliquary of glass, silver and ebony, is an arm bone of Thomas Cantilupe.

In 1664, when Fr Cuffaud was still custodian of the relics, he presented Thomas's right shin bone to a fellow Jesuit, Fr Evans, who, under the name of Fr Humphrey Brown, was the Superior of house at Holywell in North Wales. The chapel and priest's house at Holywell, despite being known as the Old Star Inn, was a most appropriate place for a sacred shin bone for it was an established pilgrimage centre, where pilgrims would come to dip their hands into the healing waters of Saint Winifred's Well.

The relic was kept at Holywell until 1835 when it was moved to the Catholic college at Stonyhurst. And there it remains and can still be seen inside a beautiful reliquary of silver and glass made by Hardman of Birmingham, engraved with 'the singular armorial bearings of the Cantilupes'.[5]

It may be that the destruction of the Lady Chapel shrine saved the original tomb in the north transept from a similar fate, both at the time of the destruction of the shrines and later during the Civil War. For after 1349, when the relics were translated to the Lady Chapel shrine, the early tomb was abandoned. The neglect soon showed.

There are several late seventeenth-century and eighteenth-century drawings which show that at one time its base was wider along the sides, perhaps allowing space for pilgrims to kneel; also the whole tomb stood closer to the wall. In 1813 it was opened; a ring, a seal and the head of a crozier were discovered inside and carefully removed. Sadly in 1838, they disappeared and have never been found.

In 1857 the tomb was dismantled and reconstructed in its present position on a smaller base. Then in 1934 it was cleaned and, according to the 1935 Annual Report, treated with a 'special preservative solution' to stop the stone from crumbling.[6] Most recently, in 1996, plans were made for a major restoration. The work was painstakingly carried out by experts and when it was completed in 1998, a special service of rededication was held on 2nd October, the feast day of Saint Thomas of Hereford.

Would it have happened without Swinfield? Without his promotion would there have been a Saint Thomas at all? Come to that how many owed their canonization more to their promoters than to their virtuous lives? Or how many missed out for lack of recognition? There was no media in medieval times. News spread by word of mouth or public proclamation. The media, as we say now, is the message; without it likely saints remained obscure.

Richard Swinfield spread Thomas's message; he handled the public relations, to use a modern term, and did so on the whole successfully – by building the tomb in the north transept, by laying plans for the great Lady Chapel shrine, by constant lobbying for canonization, above all, by the promotion of the cult.

It may also be that Swinfield employed public relations in a more subtle form. An intriguing theory put forward by Professor Valerie Flint connects the Hereford Mappa Mundi with both Swinfield and Thomas. She suggests that Swinfield used the map, made by his friend, Richard de Bello – they had been fellow clerics at Lincoln Cathedral – to promote Thomas's canonization. She points out that it is possible to interpret many details in the map as referring to Thomas; the rider in the right hand corner could be Thomas himself on his way to Orvieto; the letters M-O-R-S (death) round the border of the map could refer to his death, and the huntsmen, also at bottom right, might illustrate his bitter quarrel with Gilbert de Clare over the hunting rights on Malvern Down. Another clue can be found in the carvings of the sphynx and gryphon on the upper corners of the tomb; these two creatures can also be found in the upper corners of the map appearing remarkably similar. Professor Paul Harvey has produced convincing evidence of the map having been altered at some stage – when is unclear – to include the city of Hereford. Which, together with questions raised by more recent research about the origins of the map, suggesting it may have been made at Hereford, make Professor Flint's theory more credible.

Another possible connection between Thomas and the map can be found in the cathedral chair made for the visit of King Stephen in 1138, and the throne pictured at the bottom left of the map. The carving on the outer uprights of the back of the throne match the carving on the uprights of the Cathedral chair. Seated on the throne is an episcopal figure generally thought to be the Emperor Augustus. If Professor Flint's theory is true, it could be Pope Gregory X who presided over the second Council of Lyons in 1274 at which Thomas was present. Or could the figure be Bishop Cantilupe himself?

What is hard to tell, and we shall never know, is whether Swinfield was more concerned with enriching the cathedral or with having his predecessor canonized. He is known to have been devoted to Thomas, to have admired him greatly, as seems to have been true of those who knew him well; Robert of Gloucester, Robert Wych, Hugh le Barber, Robert Deynte; there were many more. Yet Thomas was not without his critics, enemies even, the allies of Pecham, a number of the Aquablanca clan. He often came across as cold, a dour academic who held himself aloof, who lacked the human touch, who lacked sympathy. He was condemned for being a pluralist, for pursuing litigation so relentlessly that he would stoop to bribery to win his cause. And so he did. In defence of human rights and the rights of the Church, he judged such action to be justified.

But if he was cold and unapproachable, why did crowds of pilgrims visit his shrine? Simply to be cured is the obvious answer. Less easy to explain is why people went to meet him as he rode past on his palfrey, bringing their children to be blessed or confirmed. It would seem, too, that despite his reputation for discipline, he was generally welcomed when he made his visitations. Admittedly he was generous, always bringing presents for the neediest, but he also brought his blessing and the love of God. People wanted that, they believed in it.

Hugh le Barber said Thomas had the face of an angel, meaning, perhaps, he was in touch with God. Which might explain why he wept as he celebrated Mass.

So how do we read this complicated priest? An

inflexible disciplinarian with, were there such a thing, a master's degree in self-denial; efficient, conscientious, generous, a man of outstanding sanctity who was able to inspire widespread devotion. But though all these qualities are true of him, seven centuries on we seem a long way from understanding the last Englishman to be canonized before the Reformation.

Perhaps the most telling story about him is that once – by Swinfield's reckoning it was 1277 – when he was celebrating Mass in the chapel of the Duke of Cornwall's castle at Wallingford, birds flew to the window at the sound of his voice. When he was silent they flew away, but as he began to sing again, back they came.

The story was believed, that is its significance. People accepted that Thomas was a man of such holiness that even small birds were drawn to him.

In their minds there was no doubt. Thomas Cantilupe was a rightful saint.

NOTES

Chapter I

1. The word 'cult' refers to the belief in the holiness and miraculous power of a particular dead person and the resulting devotion shown by his or her followers in various ways such as pilgrimages to their tomb or shrine, the offering of gifts.
2. Of the several meanings of the word 'gest' in this case 'heroic deed' seems nearest the mark.
3. The generally accepted date of Thomas's birth is based on Richard Swinfield's evidence at the canonization enquiry stating that Thomas was aged sixty-three 'or a little more' when he died in August 1282.
4. See J. M. Ferrante *Women as image in medieval literature from the twelfth century to Dante* (Columbia University Press, New York, 1975).
5. See *Sancti Bernard Vita Prima PL.* vol. 185 col. 257.
6. See *The Life of Saint Anselm, Archbishop of Canterbury by Eadner* edited and translated by R. W. Southern (Nelson Series, London, 1962), pp. 37–39.

7. *De Eodum et Diverso* ed. H. Wilner, *Beitridge zur Geschite des Mittelalters*, 4 (1906)
8. A. E. Bernstein, 'Theology between Heresy and Folklore': William of Auvergne on Punishment after Death, *Studies in Medieval and Renaissance History*, 5 (1982), p. 29 and note 80.
9. Thomas would have made his first confession at an early age, certainly before taking his first communion. And, though children were usually confirmed in their infancy, Fr Illtud Barrett suggests that Thomas was probably eleven or twelve years old, at an age when he understood its full meaning.
10. Lamprey: an eel-like type of fish with a round, sucking mouth that moves from the sea to fresh water to breed.
11. Philip of Novare, *Les Quatre Ages de l'homme*, ed. M. de Ereville (Paris 1888), s.20, pp. 13–14, p. 23 (ch. IV i (note 31 Red Book p. 64).
12. Chivalry, the knightly culture of medieval Europe, was based on the concepts of courtesy and honour as exemplified in the Arthurian legend. A young squire was accepted into the order of chivalry following his induction into knighthood. This solemn ritual, which generally followed a day of boisterous revels with his friends, began with bathing then dressing in white garments with a red robe. After this came the blessing of his sword which was laid on the chapel altar before which he kept vigil through the night, praying for the purification of his soul. At dawn there was confession followed by the Mass then, entering the lists and to accompanying music, the young man would be dressed by his fellow knights in his armour, helmet and, most symboli-

cally, his spurs. His sword, brought from the altar to be used for the dubbing, would be administered, probably by his father, with a meaningful whack.

Chapter II

1. Grosseteste *Epistolate, i,* pp. 75 and 162, Wilkins *Concilia, i,* pp. 635–40.
2. *Dictionary of National Biography* (see footnote p. 2).
3. Anthony Wood *The History of Antiquities of Oxford* (ed. J. Gutch, Oxford, 1792–6), I, p. 221.
4. In the first half of the thirteenth century, before the founding of individual colleges, students at Oxford University lodged in boarding houses, attending lectures in hired halls and churches. The earliest colleges were University, 1249, Balliol, 1263, then Merton, 1264. It was later that the practice of dining in hall became gradually established.
5. The word 'canon' is derived from the Greek *kanon* meaning a straight rod or bar, i.e. something fixed and so a rule or norm. In church usage this applies to the canon of the scripture, the canon of the Mass, or the declaring of a person to be among the canon of the saints, i.e. canonization.
6. *Acta Sanctorum,* Octobris, I, 545.
7. C. Lefebre in *Dictionaire de droit canonique,* s.n. Hostiensis, V, i211–27.
8. A quarter equalled eight bushels or four pecks or a fourth part of a wagon load, the size of which depended considerably on the generosity of the supplier.
9. Simon de Montfort, a high-born Norman, came to England as a young man to claim his inherited

title to the Earldom of Leicester. With intelligence, ambition and considerable charm, he soon established himself at court, becoming close friends with Henry III; they were about the same age. However Simon's marriage, in secret, to Henry's sister, Eleanor, caused the first of many rifts between them. As Simon became increasingly powerful their relationship deteriorated.

10. Emden, I, 347–9; *Medieval Archives of the University of Oxford*, ed. H. E. Salter, Oxford Historical Society (Oxford, 1917–19), I, 23–4.

11. Wood, *History.*, I, p. 258 (Gutch). The English is from the medieval rhyme:

Chronic si penses, cum pugnant Oxienses,
Post paucos menses volat ira per Anglinses.

Chapter III

1. Originally a mark was the measurement by weight of pure silver. In England after the Conquest the ratio of twenty sterling pennies to an ounce was the basis of computation. Hence the value of the mark became fixed at 160 pence, that is 13 shillings and four pence or two-thirds of the pound sterling.

2. Matthew Paris, born about 1200, became a monk of the Benedictine abbey of Saint Albans in 1217 and was a member of the court of Henry III. His extensive coverage of the years 1235 to 1259 form the second part of his major work, the *Chronica Majora*, a history of the world from the Creation to 1259.

3. The word 'parliament', an assembly to make parley, was a new name first mentioned by Matthew Paris in 1246 (M. Paris, *Chron. Maj.*) for

the type of gathering introduced after the first Magna Carta at which the king met his barons to discuss the business of the realm.

See also Powicke, *The Thirteenth Century, 1216–1307*, 1953 edition, pp. 344–7.

4. M. Paris *Chron. Maj.*
5. *Cronica Majorum*, ed. Stapleton.

Chapter IV

1. *Calendar of Patent Rolls 1258–56, 416; Calendar of Liberate Rolls 1260–7, p. 169.*
2. Powicke, *The Thirteenth Century 1216–1307*, 1964 edition.
3. *Close Rolls* 1264–8, 55, p. 62.
4. *Flores Historiarum*, ed. H. R. Luard (Rolls Series, 1890); III, p. 9.
5. *The Metrical Chronicle of Robert of Gloucester*, ed W. A. Wright. (Rolls Series, London, 1887).

Chapter V

1. The influence of the Pope and his legates and the part they played in English affairs had greatly increased since King John made England a fief of the Holy See. From that time, the Pope had been the King's overlord. As Fr Illtud Barrett points out, on the whole, papal interest was favourable to the Crown – something for which Henry III was profoundly grateful.
2. The grant of safe conduct came three weeks after Easter. It was the following year, on 10th February 1266, that Thomas received letters admitting him to grace and forgiveness. *Calendar of Patent Rolls 1285–66*, p. 443, p. 549, p. 596.
3. Canon Capes notes that Thomas bought Montalt,

195

the house in Old Fish Street Hill from the Montalt family and left it for the use of his successors. Certainly Richard Swinfield made use of it as his register shows.

4. *The Wardrobe and Household Account of Bogo de Clare 1284–6*, ed. M. S. Guiseppi, in *Archeologia*, vol. lxx, Opus 31. The account includes a record of 70s spent on ginger. At that time the standard annual wage for a stipendiary chaplain was 66s 8d.

5. The origin of tithe can be found in Genesis 28:22.

Chapter VI

1. *Register of W. Giffard* pp. 278–86. This gives a list of about three hundred who gave money for crusades, of whom one hundred and fifteen were priests. Of the priests thirty-nine are listed as crusaders, *crucesignati*, but many may never have actually set sail.

2. *Acta Sanctorum*, Octobris, I, p. 545.

3. Wood, *op. cit.*, I, p. 65.

4. In the Middle Ages a prebend supplied or furnished (*praebere*) its holder, who became known as a prebendary, with a living normally consisting of the revenue from one manor of the cathedral estates. Most prebendaries were also canons with a stall in the cathedral. By the nineteenth century a prebend, in almost all cases, had become an honorary position carrying with it simply a stall in the cathedral. In the former monastic cathedrals, reorganized following the Dissolution and known as the New Foundation', the title 'Prebend' has generally been replaced by 'Canon'. Hereford, being a cathedral of the Old

Foundation' (with no monastic connection) has retained the title of 'Prebend'.

5. *Acta Sanctorum*, p. 500.

Chapter VII

1. Vat. Cod. Lat. 4015, folio 78.
2. *A roll of the Household Expenses of R. Swinfield during part of the years 1289–90*, ed. John Webb, Camden Society, 2 vols. 1854–5 shows the extent of a thirteenth-century bishop's entourage.
3. Matthew Paris wrote 'Anglicum idioma ignoravit': *Chron. Maj. v*, p. 422.
4. See e.g. *Regist. T. Corbridge*, i, p. 95; *Regist. W. Wickwayn*, pp. 93, 126; *egist. J. Pecham* (C. and Y. Soc.) pp. 139–64.
5. By the statutes of the Council of Lambeth, 1261, every bishop was required to provide himself with one or two prisons in his diocese. If a prisoner escaped the bishop was liable to a fine of one hundred pounds.
   Wilkins, *Concilia*, i, p. 755; cf. *Regist. J. Pontissara*, pp. 461–2.
   Pecham, *Regist. Epist.* iii, p. 914.
   Gabel, *Benefit of Clergy*, p. 111.
6. *Acta Sanctorum*, p. 547–8.
7. In his biography of Edward I, Michael Prestwich described Thomas's reaction as 'a violent and hysterical outburst' adding that Thomas 'threatened to resign from the council'.
   Acta Sanctorum, Octobris, ed. J. Bollandus, i (Paris, Rome, 1866) pp. 474–5.
8. *Acta Sanctorum*, p. 511.
9. *Acta Sanctorum*, p. 513.

1. In the twelfth century synods had been largely concerned with judicial matters and were therefore attended by both laity and clergy. By the thirteenth century they had become more concerned with church legislation and were therefore generally confined to the clergy. See C. R. Cheney, *English Synodalia of the Thirteenth Century*, p. 33.

2. *A Roll of the Household Expenses of Richard de Swinfield during part of the years 1280–90*, ed. John Webb, Camden Society, 2 vols. 1854–5.

3. Some of the questionnaires have been preserved: see *W. Giffard*, pp. 26–8.

4. *Acta Sanctorum*, October, i, p. 561. At the Council of Oxford in 1222 it was stated that parents must not wait too long for the coming of the bishop but must take their children to him, when he is known to be in the neighbourhood, as quickly as possible.

5. Acolytes were one of the four Minor Orders of the Catholic Church, i.e. those graded below that of deacon. The other three were: doorkeepers, lectors and exorcists. The grade of subdeacon had been upgraded from a Minor Order in 1207.

6. Ember Days are listed as Wednesdays, Fridays and Saturdays after the first Sunday in Lent, Whitsunday, Holy Cross Day, 14th September, and Saint Lucia's Day, 13th December. However, according to records, Thomas held ordinations at other times as well.

7. See L. J. Dobson, *The Origins of Ancrene Wisse*, Oxford 1976. Included in the works are dramatic dialogues based on the lives of female saints, which must be among the earliest of medieval mystery plays.

8. *Registrum Epistolarum Fratris Johannes, archiepiscopi Cantuariensis*, ed. C. T. Martin, Rolls Series, 3 vols., (1882–5, II, pp. 505–7).

Chapter IX

1. Powicke *The Thirteenth Century 1216–1307*, p. 489.
2. See the Preface of *The Life and Gests of Saint Thomas Cantilupe* by Richard Strange, 1879 edition.
3. Grosseteste *P. Epistolate*, ed. H. R. Luard.
4. There are seven daily 'hours', fixed times appointed for prayer, e.g. Matins, early in the morning, Nones said at the ninth hour, Vespers in the evening.
5. The Court of Arches at Saint Mary-le-Bow, or de Arcubus, supposedly takes its name from the stone arches of the eleventh-century crypt. Though badly damaged in the Great Fire in 1666, part of its distinctive steeple survived. The church was rebuilt by Sir Christopher Wren.
6. See Canon Capes's introduction to *The Register of Thomas de Cantilupe*, p. xlviii, note 6.
7. See *Saint Thomas Cantilupe, Bishop of Hereford. Essays in his honour*, pp. 103–23.

Chapter X

1. The account roll of Thomas's last journey is roughly sixteen centimetres wide and over a metre long.
2. The handwriting of the Edwardian period, 1270–1330, can best be identified by the upright letters which, rather than standing straight, loop over in an elaborate curl like a beaver's tail.
3. *Reg, Peckham*, R. S., I, pp. 318–20.
4. According to the historian, Robert Brentano,

Adam of Fileby, a canon of Hereford, was 'the most notorious of the late thirteenth-century English curial proctors'.
5. On 19th January 1282, Pecham had written to Chioletti asking for support.
   Reg. Peckham, R. S., I. pp. 282–3, Vat. Cod. Lat. 4016 folios.
6. fos. 32r, 35r, 9r.
7. fos. 32v; *cf.* 9v. From this reference it is suggested that this meeting took place at Montefiascone following Pope Martin's move to his other papal residence.
8. fos. 101v, 62v.

Chapter XI

1. Documents concerning Pecham's proposed visit are included in his register. *Register Peckham*, RS., II, p. 421, pp. 430–431, p. 478, pp. 484–6; Reg. *Peckham*, C and Y., LXV, p. 177.
   Also in *Calendar of Hereford Archives*, II, p. 562.
2. For references to Edith's and other miracles see *Acta Sanctorum*, pp. 632–3, p. 636, pp. 697–8.
3. For full details of the tomb see G. Marshall 'The shrine of Saint Thomas de Cantilupe in Hereford Cathedral' in *Trans. Woolhope Naturalists Field Club*, XXVII, (1930–32), pp. 34–50; and E. G. Benson 'The lost brass of the Cantilupe shrine' in *Trans. W.N.F.C.* (1949–51), pp. 68–76.

Chapter XII

1. *Reg. Swinfield*, pp. 440–41, pp. 420–21.
2. A detailed account of the enquiry based on research into Vatican records has been made by Patrick H. Daly and can be found in *Saint*

Thomas Cantilupe, Bishop of Hereford, Essays in his Honour.

3. Having been the church of a Benedictine monastery for almost 450 years the great abbey at Gloucester became a cathedral in 1541.

4. Dom Benet Gibbon's 1720 account of Thomas Cantilupe's skull is in the Downside Archives.

5. J. Morris, 'English relics, I; Saint Thomas of Hereford', *The Month*, XLIV (Jan.–Apr., 1882), pp. 125–6. See R.C. Finucane, *Miracles and Pilgrims*, plate 15, for a photograph of this relic.

6. The 1935 Annual Report of the Friends of Hereford Cathedral states that the tomb had been treated with preservative solution in 1934 'thus fixing the crumbling particles and making it safe for many years to come'.

BIBLIOGRAPHY

Saint Thomas Cantilupe, Bishop of Hereford, Essays in his Honour edited by Meryl Jancey. Published by The Friends of Hereford Cathedral, Publications Committee, 1982.

The Register of Thomas de Cantilupe transcribed by Rev. R. G. Griffiths with an introduction by Rev. W. W. Capes. Printed by Wilson and Phillips, Printers, High St., Hereford, 1906.

The Life and Gests of Saint Thomas Cantilupe by Richard Strange. Printed by Robert Walker at the signe of the Annunciation of our Blessed Lady, 1674.

Reissued as *The Life of Saint Thomas of Hereford* by Richard Strange. Printed by Burns and Oates, Burns St and Paternoster Row, 1879.

Kings, Barons and Serfs, A Pictorial History 1086–1300, by R. J. Unstead. Published by Macdonald Educational, 1971.

The Clergy Review (Periodical) August 1947, Vol. xxviii, No. 2. Published by Burns, Oates and Washbourne Ltd.

Friends of Hereford Cathedral Annual Records, Nov. 1935. Printed by the *Hereford Times*, Ltd, Hereford.

London City Churches, by Gerald Cobb. Published by B. T. Batsford, London, 1977. Revised by Nicholas Redman, 1989.

Edward I by Michael Prestwich. Published by Methuen, London Ltd., 1988.

Childhood in the Middle Ages by Shulamith Shahar. Published by Routledge, London, 1990.

The Encyclopedia of Religion. Published by Macmillan, 1987.

The Thirteenth Century, 1216–1307 by Sir Maurice Powicke. Published by Oxford at the Clarendon Press, 1953. Republished by O.U.P. (Readers' Union) 1964.

Hereford Cathedral by George Marshall F.S.A. Published by the Worcester Press (no date).

Miracles and Pilgrims by Ronald C. Finucane. Published by J. M. Dent and Sons Ltd., 1977.

The Medieval English Economy by J. L. Bolton. Published by J. M. Dent and Sons Ltd., 1980.

Dictionary of National Biography V.III edited by Sir Leslie Stephens. Published by O.U.P. from 1917. Reprinted 1937–8.

The Oxford Dictionary of the Christian Church edited by F. L. Cross. Published by O.U.P., 1957.

Saint Thomas of Hereford by E. M. Jancey. Published by Hereford Cathedral Publications, 1978.

England in the XIII Century by Alan Harding. Published by Cambridge University Press, 1993.

Church Life in England in the Thirteen Century by John R. H. Moorman. Published by Cambridge University Press, 1946.

THE HEREFORD

MAPPA MUNDI

A MEDIEVAL VIEW OF THE WORLD

Gabriel Alington

Illustrations by
Dominic Harbour

The Mappa Mundi gives us today an incomparable insight into the mind of Medieval Christendom, depicting not only the geographical world but also the spirituality, philosophy of life and the political and economic structures of its people. The creation of such a map was not only a considerable achievement, but a symbol of power and status in a world still in a feudal state. This volume takes the reader on a tour of that world as well as of the map; a journey as fascinating as the Mappa itself.

GRACE GUIDES
ON BRITISH HERITAGE

BORDERLANDS

The History
and Romance
of the
Herefordshire
Marches

Wigmore

Leominster

Hereford

GABRIEL ALINGTON

Illustrations by
DOMINIC HARBOUR

An attractive guide to the history of the Borders, including the burial chambers of Neolithic man, Offa's Dyke, the ruins of Llanthony Priory and Dore Abbey, the numerous forts and castles of the area, unusual churches and the forgotten priory of Limebrook.